VERY EASY

CRAZY PATCHWORK

VERY EASY
CRAZY
PATCHWORK

**All you need to know to master
freeform patchwork techniques**

BETTY BARNDEN

A QUARTO BOOK

Published by Apple Press Ltd
4th Floor
114 Western Road
Hove, BN3 1DD
www.apple-press.com

QUAR.PTW

ISBN: 978–1–84543–171–6

Conceived, designed, and produced by
Quarto Publishing plc
The Old Brewery
6 Blundell Street
London N7 9BH

SENIOR EDITOR: Liz Pasfield
ART EDITOR: Sheila Volpe
DESIGNER: Tania Field
PHOTOGRAPHERS: Philip Wilkins, Martin Norris
COPY EDITOR: Claire Waite Brown
ILLUSTRATORS: Elsa Godfrey, Coral Mula
ASSISTANT ART DIRECTOR: Penny Cobb

ART DIRECTOR: Moira Clinch
PUBLISHER: Paul Carslake

Manufactured by PICA Digital, Singapore
Printed in Singapore by Star Standard Industries (PTE) Ltd.

9 8 7 6 5 4 3 2 1

CONTENTS

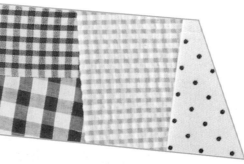

INTRODUCTION

The essence of crazy patchwork lies in gathering a collection of fabrics that you like, stitching them together, often with minimal planning, and then adding as much or as little decoration as you desire.

Crazy patchwork involves cutting irregularly shaped patches from different fabrics, and sewing them onto a fabric foundation. The patches may be secured by machine stitching, hand stitching, or embroidery stitches, and more embroidery can be added as decoration.

Early scrap quilting developed for reasons of economy. Where fabrics were scarce and relatively expensive, every scrap was precious, and thrifty needlewomen would naturally devise ways of stitching such scraps together for bed quilts and even curtains. Pre-Victorian examples that survive today are mainly from America, but examples also exist from other countries, such as Australia. The purpose of such needlework was strictly utilitarian, but even so, there was still an element of choice in the fitting together of remnants of different colours and textures.

During the nineteenth century many developments influenced needlework. Industrial textile machinery produced cotton and wool fabrics by the mile that were cheaper and in greater variety than ever before, and the sewing machine was invented. Steamships and railways made these products available all around the world and carried Chinese silks and Indian cottons from East to West. In the Victorian era crazy quilts were made in both America and Europe, using fancy fabrics such as prints, silks, satins and velvets. The patches were usually secured with hand embroidery and further embellished with silk and cotton threads, lace, beads and sequins. Crazy patchwork became a leisure activity and an art form with unlimited possibilities for colour and composition.

Today an even greater variety of fabrics and threads is
available. We can combine colour and fabric with modern
machine stitching, which has made quilting faster and easier than ever
before. And we can decorate with as much or as little embroidery as we
choose. But because our leisure time is often limited, smaller projects, such as
purses and pillows, are often more popular than bed quilts.

There are several ways of constructing crazy patchwork, some speedier than others. The
techniques and projects in this book are arranged in order of difficulty. As you try out
each technique, you can make the project that follows. Use this book to help you
discover which methods of composition and construction you enjoy, and the type of
decoration that works best for you.

Your own versions of the projects in this book will be unique to you. Your collection of
scrap fabrics expresses your taste, and if you search fabric and quilt shops and the
Internet, the choices you make will also express your own personality. Make beautiful gifts
for your friends and family or colourful household articles for your home, all totally
unique and with your own creative signature.

Happy stitching!

Betty Barnden

Chapter 1

STITCHING KNOW-HOW

Only a few basic sewing techniques are needed to assemble crazy-patchwork projects and basic embroidery techniques can be applied across a wide range of different stitches. Whether you prefer to stitch by hand or by machine, follow these simple guidelines for perfect results every time.

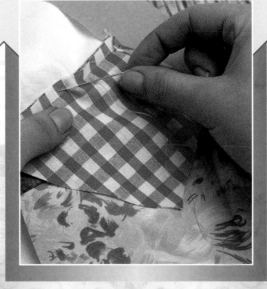

HAND-SEWING AND EMBROIDERY EQUIPMENT

You will need a selection of basic tools, some of which you may already own. In general, equipment for hand sewing and embroidery is not expensive, and you can purchase new items as the need arises. If you need to make a purchase, always buy the best quality you can afford, since inexpensive items do not always do the job well. Cheap scissors, for example, rarely cut cleanly and the blades may work loose, while good-quality scissors can last a lifetime.

NEEDLES

Needles should be chosen to suit the weight of the fabric and thread you intend to use. Whether you are sewing seams by hand or working embroidery, the needle should be fine enough to pass easily through the fabric, and at the same time the eye should be large enough to hold the thread. Different types of needles are used for different purposes. Within each type the needles are sized by number — the higher the number, the smaller and finer the needle.

GENERAL-PURPOSE NEEDLES
Sometimes called household needles, or sharps, these needles are for general-purpose sewing, such as sewing seams and hems. They have a short, round eye suitable for all types of sewing thread and are sized from 1 to 12. A pack of assorted sizes will suit most projects.

EMBROIDERY NEEDLES
Embroidery needles are sometimes called crewel needles, and are similar to general-purpose needles but with a slim, elongated eye to take one or more threads of cotton embroidery thread or similar thread. They are available in sizes 1 to 10 to suit many different weights of thread.

BETWEENS
These are very short, sharp needles for quick, even stitching. Sized from 1 to 10, sizes 5 to 8 will suit most quilted projects. You can also use them for sewing seams and hems.

CHENILLE NEEDLES
These are heavier than embroidery needles but quite short, and with a larger eye. Use them for embroidery with heavier threads, such as pearl cotton and soft cotton. Available in sizes 13 to 26, the smaller sizes (18 to 26) are most useful for embroidery. A large size (13 or 14) can be used to finish off a laid thread when couching.

TAPESTRY NEEDLES
Tapestry needles are just like chenille needles, but with a blunt tip. Use them for working certain embroidery techniques, such as whipping, when the blunt tip will prevent the needle from piercing the fabric or the previous stitching. The largest size (13) can be used to thread cord or ribbon through a casing.

PINS

Pins are used to hold fabrics in place while stitching them together. You will need a selection of different sizes.

DRESSMAKER'S PINS

Tempered steel pins are available in a range of sizes to suit different weights of fabric: The lighter the fabric, the finer the pins. Choose a medium size for most crazy-patchwork projects.

GLASS-HEADED PINS

Glass-headed pins are useful for large projects that use heavy fabrics. The coloured heads make the pins easy to spot and remove when machine stitching. Extra long glass-headed pins are useful for pinning together the layers of a quilted article.

THIMBLES

Using a thimble enables you to push the needle through the fabric with ease, saving wear and tear on your fingers.

SEWING THIMBLE

Wear an ordinary sewing thimble to avoid pricking the second finger of your sewing hand when sewing or embroidering. Choose a size that fits comfortably.

QUILTER'S THIMBLE

A special quilting thimble has a ridge around the crown to help push the needle through all the layers of the quilt without slipping.

EMBROIDERY HOOPS

Adjustable wooden embroidery hoops are available in various sizes and are used to stretch the work flat while embroidering, and to prevent puckering. For couching and quilting, use a hoop in a stand to leave both hands free.

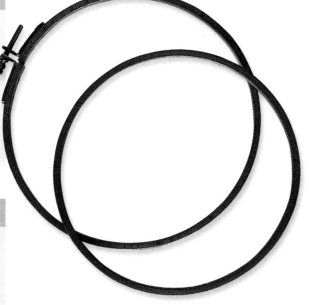

IRON

An ordinary steam iron is essential for pressing fabrics flat and for pressing seams as you sew. Keep the base plate clean, as recommended by the manufacturer. It is a good idea to set up your ironing table right next to your worktable. A small travel iron is useful for pressing small details, such as ruffles and rosettes.

CUTTING EQUIPMENT

Using the right tool for the job makes clean, accurate cutting easy.

PAPER SCISSORS

A medium-sized pair of scissors is useful for cutting paper and template plastic. Never use dressmaker's shears for this purpose, because they will become dull very quickly.

DRESSMAKER'S SHEARS

Dressmaker's shears are quite large, with a flat lower edge on the lower blade that rests on the work surface as the fabric is cut. The handles are moulded to fit the thumb and fingers, and angled to give the correct cutting position. Keep these shears exclusively for cutting fabric. Left-handed versions are also available.

SMALL, SHARP SCISSORS

Keep a pair of small, sharp scissors on hand for cutting threads when sewing or working embroidery stitches. These are also useful for snipping notches and other small details.

SEAM RIPPER

A seam ripper is invaluable for removing unwanted stitches quickly and neatly.

MEASURING AND MARKING TOOLS

Accurate measuring and marking is the key to assembling any project neatly and with ease.

FABRIC MARKERS

An erasable fabric-marking pen makes a mark (often blue) that can be removed by misting or rinsing with water. On fabrics where a blue line will not show, use a quilter's pencil – available in colours such as yellow and silver – and remove the chalk marks by brushing.

ACRYLIC SQUARE

A right-angled set square is invaluable for drawing block outlines and making accurate templates.

TAPE MEASURE

A cloth tape measure is useful for measuring fabric. Buy a new one occasionally, because the first few centimetres tend to stretch after a while.

RULER

Use a clear plastic ruler to help you draw straight, accurate guidelines for both cutting and embroidery. A longer ruler, of 60–100 cm (2–3 ft), is advantageous for many projects.

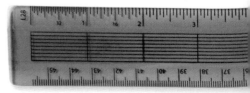

SEWING AND
HAND-EMBROIDERY THREADS

Choosing the right thread is as important as choosing fabrics. Getting to know the different types available, and when to use them, will make your stitching quicker and easier to work. Sewing threads are used for sewing seams and hems by hand or machine, and embroidery threads are available in a wide variety of types for hand embroidery. Special machine-embroidery threads, which are fine, smooth, and strong, are sold on spools for machine work (see page 15).

SEWING THREADS

Choosing the right sewing thread to suit the job in hand is essential to the success of your crazy-patchwork project.

GENERAL-PURPOSE SEWING THREADS

As a general rule, 100 per cent cotton sewing thread is the best choice for crazy-patchwork seams, assembly seams and hems. Polyester and polyester/cotton blends are also available and are often used for sewing synthetic fabrics. Silk thread should be used when sewing silk fabrics. All these thread types are suitable for both hand and machine stitching.

QUILTING THREAD

Quilting thread is heavier and stronger than general-purpose sewing thread and has a waxed finish to promote smooth stitching, whether by hand or machine.

HAND-EMBROIDERY THREADS

There are many different types of embroidery thread available, each with their own characteristics. The beginner will find cotton thread and pearl cotton No. 5 the easiest to work with, but other, more unusual threads, such as silks and metallics, will provide a unique look to your work.

COTTON EMBROIDERY THREAD

Cotton embroidery thread comes in small skeins, with six strands loosely wound together. The strands can be separated and combined to make up any weight of thread required, making it suitable for any size project. Cotton embroidery thread is widely available in a huge range of colours, both plain and shade-dyed.

SILK EMBROIDERY THREAD

Silk thread is similar in weight to cotton thread and used in the same way. Silk thread is expensive, but the subtle glow of coloured silks adds a touch of luxury to your work.

PEARL COTTON

This twisted, rounded thread is heavier than cotton embroidery thread, and the strands may not be separated. Again, a wide range of colours is available in several weights: No. 5 is the most common, while No. 3 is heavier, and Nos. 8 and 12 are finer. Use pearl cotton for bold embroidery on medium to large projects.

COTON À BRODER

This fine, twisted thread has a matt finish and may not be separated into strands. It is very easy to use, defining stitches neatly, and suitable for small to medium projects.

SOFT EMBROIDERY COTTON

This soft, rounded heavy thread has a matte finish and may not be separated into finer strands. Use this thread for bold stitching on large projects or for couching (see page 122).

METALLIC THREADS

Many different types of metallic thread are available for hand embroidery to add sparkle to your work.

VISCOSE RAYON THREADS

Viscose rayon thread is available in several weights, on spools or in skeins. It is sometimes difficult to handle, but the high-gloss finish adds a touch of glamour to any project.

SEWING-MACHINE WORK

A sewing machine is not a requirement for most of the projects in this book, but even the most basic model will speed up your work and enable you to assemble projects in a fraction of the time it would take to sew them by hand. The threads used for sewing seams and hems are the same as for hand sewing (see page 13), but to embroider by machine, you will need specific machine-embroidery threads.

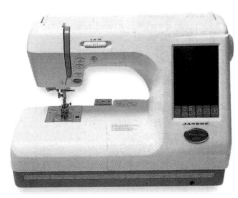

SEWING MACHINE

Your sewing machine needs to be capable of only straight stitch and zigzag stitch. A machine with automatic embroidery stitches will, however, give you the opportunity to add fast, accurate embellishments to your projects.

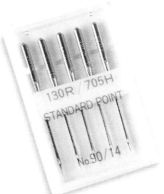

SEWING-MACHINE NEEDLES

Machine needles quickly become dull, so change the needle after every project or two. Different needle sizes are available to suit different fabric weights (see page 24).

MACHINE-EMBROIDERY HOOPS

Many types of machine-embroidery hoops are available; these are designed to hold the stretched fabric flat on the sewing-machine bed. This spring hoop is very shallow, so it will slide under the lifted presser foot of most sewing machines. It may also be repositioned while the work is under the presser foot (with the needle down), which saves time.

MACHINE-EMBROIDERY THREADS

A wide range of machine-embroidery threads is available, such as 100 per cent cotton (slightly heavier than sewing thread), glossy viscose rayon threads, and metallic threads. Choose from the wide range of plain and variegated colours.

SPECIAL FABRIC PRODUCTS

In addition to the types of fabrics shown in the Fabric Directory (see page 138), there are various other fabric products with specific uses that you may want to become familiar with. Many of these products are described as "non-woven," meaning that the fibres are compressed into a sheet rather than woven together.

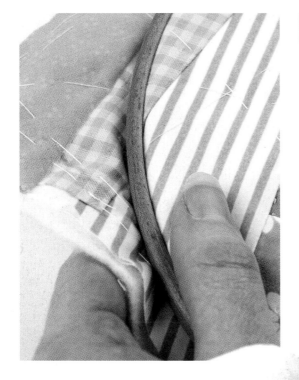

WADDING

Wadding is used as the middle layer between the top and bottom fabric layers of a quilted project, throwing the quilted design into relief. Wadding also adds a warm insulating layer to a project, such as a bed quilt. Various wadding types are available in a variety of weights – from 60 g (2 oz.) to 220 g (8 oz.) – to suit different projects. Low-loft wadding is flatter and drapes better than the high-loft variety, which has a puffier appearance.

POLYESTER WADDING

Choose a light weight for hand or machine quilting, and opt for heavier weights for tied or button quilting.

100 PER CENT COTTON WADDING

This type of wadding must be closely stitched, otherwise the fibres will tend to move around and form lumps.

COTTON/POLYESTER BLENDS

Cotton/polyester blends give the coolness and feel of cotton but are easier to handle than pure cotton wadding.

NEEDLEPUNCH WADDING

This is a low-loft polyester wadding that has been flattened to make it hang well. It is especially suitable for wall hangings.

Various types of waddings are available in qualities to suit all applications.

OTHER SPECIAL PRODUCTS

Today there are many new products designed to aid the creative stitcher. Such products come with full instructions and suggestions for ways to use them, so try them out for yourself and see where they lead. Here are three of the most useful products for crazy patchwork.

WATER-SOLUBLE PAPER

This product is invaluable for adding embroidered designs to crazy patchwork on a washable article. A design can be traced lightly in pencil onto the paper, or the paper can be run through a photocopier or printer using light grey rather than black ink. The paper is then tacked to the right side of the fabric and the embroidery is stitched through it by hand or machine. The paper can then be dissolved in water following the manufacturer's instructions. It can also be used as a stabilizer for machine embroidery.

SELF-ADHESIVE STABILIZER

This self-adhesive non-woven fabric comes with a peel-off paper backing. It is applied to the wrong side of the work to prevent puckering and distortion when working hand or machine embroidery on lightweight fabrics. Use it instead of an embroidery hoop, or together with a hoop for slippery fabrics. When working machine embroidery from the wrong side, the design can be traced onto the stabilizer. When the embroidery is complete, excess stabilizer should be peeled away.

FUSIBLE WEB

This non-woven fabric melts when heated with an iron and is used to permanently bond two layers of fabric together. The process stiffens the fabrics, making a firm surface that is ideal for machine embroidery. The fabrics used with fusible web must be able to withstand a hot steam iron.

FABRIC PREPARATION

Your crazy-patchwork projects will have a neater finish and a longer life if you take the time to prepare your fabrics carefully before you begin to sew.

Washing and Pressing

Take the time to wash all of the fabrics you are going to use for a project before you begin. This is especially important if using delicate fabrics or those with unknown fibre content. This will help prevent uneven shrinkage in the completed article when it is washed in the future. New fabrics are sometimes stiffened with sizing, which needs to be removed by washing. Scrap fabrics benefit from rewashing, especially if they have been in storage for some time. Always press fabrics flat after washing.

1 Wash each of your fabrics by hand, one at a time, in warm, soapy water. If any of the colours run, place that fabric aside and try the colourfastness test described below. Rinse the washed fabric well in three changes of cool water, and gently squeeze out the excess water and leave the fabric in a flat position to dry.

COLOURFASTNESS TEST

To test whether a fabric is colourfast or not, snip off a small piece and soak it in hot soapy water for two to three minutes. Now lay the fabric flat on a sheet of kitchen towel and leave to dry. Remove the fabric from the towel. If the kitchen towel is stained with even the slightest trace of colour, the fabric is not colourfast and should not be used for your patchwork projects.

2 Set your iron to the heat setting suitable for your fabrics and press them until they are flat. If you are in any doubt as to which setting to use, start by pressing a corner of the fabric on the coolest iron setting and gradually increase the heat. Only use steam on suitable fabrics, such as cotton or linen.

Cutting Fabric

Sharp dressmaker's shears are the perfect tool for cutting crazy patches; otherwise, choose a large pair of sharp scissors. Iron the fabric flat and lay it on a smooth surface before beginning to cut.

1 Most fabrics are woven with a "selvage" at each side edge, normally about 12–15 mm (½–¾ in.) wide. Do not incorporate these into your work, because they will not lie flat and they are difficult to stitch. Always cut them off.

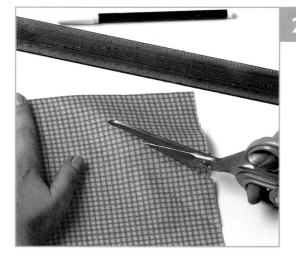

2 Crazy patches can be cut in any direction you choose. Mark the cutting lines with an erasable fabric-marking pen and ruler or draw around a template (see page 28). Use a set square to mark right-angled corners. Position the fabric so that you can make each cut away from your body rather than from side to side. Hold the fabric flat with one hand and slide the narrow blade of the dressmaker's shears under the fabric, along the tabletop. Keep the shears upright as you close the blades.

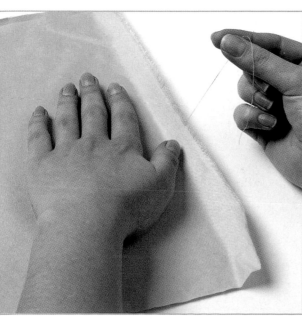

3 Whenever possible, rectangular pieces of backing fabric should be cut in alignment with the woven grain of the fabric. On fabrics with a visible weave, pull away threads from a cut edge until you find one thread that runs across the whole width, as shown, and use this line as one edge of the backing fabric you are cutting.

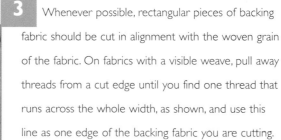

HAND SEWING

All of the crazy patchwork methods described in this book may be sewn by hand. (Some may also be done by machine, while others must be done only by hand.) Sewing by hand is slower, but it requires less equipment and can be done anywhere.

Tacking

Tacking stitches are long, straight stitches used to hold fabrics temporarily in place until they are secured with a firm seam or embroidery, after which the tacking is usually removed. Tacking is more secure than pins, and it makes the work lie flatter.

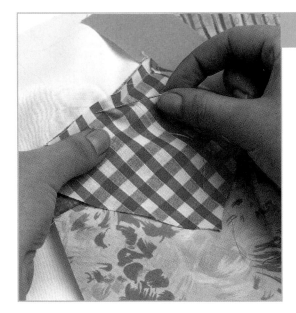

1 First, pin the seam or patch in place. Placing pins every 5 cm (2 in.) is sufficient for most fabrics. At this stage, you may want to draw a stitching line on the fabric, using a ruler and an erasable fabric-marking pen. Use sewing thread that contrasts with the fabric. Stitch up and down along the required line, making tacking stitches about 9–12 mm (⅜–½ in.) long, as shown. If you are tacking a seam, stitch just outside the stitching line so that the tacking stitches will not become caught in the permanent stitching.

2 Secure the end of the tacking thread to the fabric with two backstitches, and snip the thread tail off, as shown. After the permanent stitching is complete, you can simply unpick the backstitches and pull on the starting knot to remove the tacking stitches.

Backstitch

This hand-sewing stitch may be substituted for machine stitching when assembling a project and can be just as secure when worked correctly.

1 First tack the seam as shown on the opposite page. Although a contrasting thread has been used here for visual clarity, plan on using a thread that blends with your fabrics, remembering that an exact match is rarely possible in crazy patchwork. Don't knot the end of the thread. Begin with a small stitch of 3 mm (⅛ in.) or less on the stitching line, pulling the thread through to leave a 12-mm (½-in.) tail. Repeat this stitch in exactly the same place, as shown, then insert the needle once more in the same place, but bring it out a little farther along the line. Pull the thread through firmly.

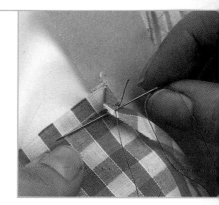

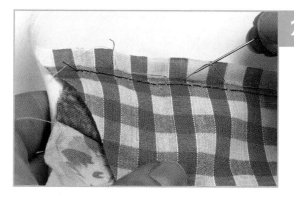

2 Insert the needle at the end of the previous stitch and bring it out again farther along the line. Pull through. Repeat this stitch as required. All the stitches should be the same length – 3 mm (⅛ in.) or less – and form a continuous line. At the end, stitch twice in the same place. Cut off the excess thread. Remove the tacking stitches, as shown.

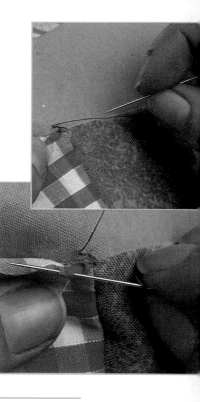

Slip Stitch

Use this stitch to sew the folded edge of a patch, as shown here, with the right side of the work facing you. You can also use this stitch to attach a lining or to close an opening in a seam after filling an item with stuffing. When worked correctly, the stitches should be practically invisible.

1 Pin and tack the patch, as shown on page 20. Match the thread colour to the fabric of the upper patch as closely as you can. Don't knot the thread end, but begin with two small backstitches under the folded edge. Take a small stitch about 3 mm (⅛ in.) long along the edge of the upper patch, inside the fold of the fabric. Pull the thread through.

2 Insert the needle into the lower patch directly opposite and take another stitch of the same size through the lower patch and through the backing fabric, as shown. Pull the thread through.

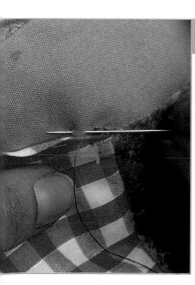

3 Repeat these two stitches, always inserting the needle directly opposite the exit point of the thread so the visible thread does not slant. The line of stitches is loose here so you can see the thread path. Pull the stitches tight. Fasten off with two tiny backstitches, either on the wrong side of the work or hidden inside a seam allowance. Remove the tacking stitches.

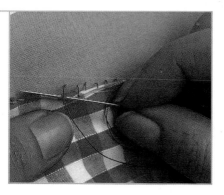

HAND EMBROIDERY

Traditionally, crazy patchwork seams are hand embroidered with a variety of stitches all in one bright colour, such as yellow or red, which unifies all of the different fabrics in the piece. However, you can use as many different colours and stitches as you like and add embroidery to the patches themselves, as well as to the seams.

Starting and Finishing Threads

1 Cut about 45 cm (18 in.) of embroidery thread. If you are using cotton or silk thread, pull out the strands one at a time and then recombine the number of strands you want to use. Thread the appropriate embroidery needle and knot one end of the thread. If you wish, you can draw lines and dots on the fabric as a guide to even stitches, using an erasable fabric-marking pen and ruler as shown.

2 Insert the needle about 7.5 cm (3 in.) away from where the stitching is to begin. Bring it up through the fabric where required. Work the desired embroidery as shown. Do not stitch outside the block outline; otherwise, the threads will be cut when you trim the work to size.

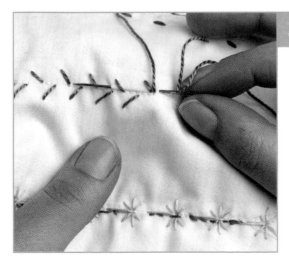

3 To end the thread, take the needle through to the wrong side and make a tiny backstitch through the backing fabric only. Run the needle between the fabric layers (or through the backs of the stitches), as shown, for about 12 mm (½ in.) before snipping the thread. Snip off the knot at the start of your work and pull the starting tail through to the wrong side. Thread it into the needle and fasten it off in the same way as above. Traces of the fabric-marking pen may be removed by misting the fabric with a water spray and leaving it to dry.

Mounting Work in a Hoop

You may prefer to stretch your work in a hoop, and for certain stitches (see Couching, page 122) it is essential to do so. Moving the hoop frequently can damage completed embroidery, so try to plan your work to move the hoop as little as possible and choose the largest hoop size that will easily take your patchwork block. You can tack strips of waste fabric to the edges of a small block so that it will fit into a large hoop.

Adjust the outer hoop ring (by means of the screw) so that it fits easily over the inner ring. Lay the inner ring on a flat surface, with the work over it, and push the outer ring into place. Never adjust the outer ring with the work in place; this can damage the fabric. Always remove the hoop, adjust the screw, and replace the ring. To remove the hoop, push gently with your thumbs on the inner ring. Always remove the hoop when you put your work aside; never leave it in the hoop, because this may stretch or mark your work permanently.

SPECIAL NOTES

■ In theory you could add hand embroidery at any stage of your project, but as a rule, it is easiest to work the embroidery before trimming your block to its final size before assembly.

■ Choose an embroidery needle and suitable thread from the table below. The needle eye should be large enough to take the thread easily and carry it smoothly through the fabric.

Fabric weight, plus suitable backing fabric	Thread type, or substitute equivalent thickness	Needle type and size
Lightweight silks or fine cottons	Two or three strands of cotton thread One or two strands of silk thread	Crewel, size 7–10
Medium-weight cotton, linen or silk dupion	Four to six strands of cotton thread Three or four strands of silk thread Cotton à broder Flower thread Pearl cotton No. 5	Crewel, size 3–6
Medium-weight coarse linen, wool or matka silk	Pearl cotton No. 3 or 5 Soft cotton	Chenille, size 13–18

SEE ALSO

■ Hand-embroidery Stitches, page 108
■ Hand Sewing, page 20

MACHINE SEWING

A basic sewing machine with straight-stitch and zigzag capability and reverse control will speed up the patching and assembly process of any project in this book. Many of today's machines can also produce beautiful embroidery stitches (see pages 26 and 134).

SPECIAL NOTES

■ Sewing machines differ, so consult your manual for basic operating procedures and identification of the controls.

■ Choose a needle size and stitch length to suit your fabrics, using the table below.

Fabric	Stitch length	European needle size	U.S. needle size
Lightweight cottons, polycottons, silks	2.5-3 mm (8–10 stitches per inch)	70–80	9–11
Medium-weight linens, twill, light denim, cottons	3-3.5 mm (7–9 stitches per inch)	80–90	11–14

Straight Stitch

This is the basic machine stitch used for many crazy-patchwork techniques and also for assembling projects.

1 Thread the machine and bobbin as instructed in your machine's manual. It is always a good idea to test the machine settings before you begin to sew. To do this, layer scraps of the same fabrics you wish to sew, and stitch a few inches through all layers. Look at both sides of the test piece to check the following:

■ If loops of the top thread (pink in photo) appear on the underside of your fabrics as shown at the far left, the top thread tension is too loose. Identify the thread tension control on your machine, tighten it by one or two settings and stitch again.
■ If the fabric puckers, as shown at centre left, or the thread breaks when the seam is pressed flat, the top thread tension is too tight. Loosen it slightly and try again.
■ If the stitches look the same on both sides and the fabric is unpuckered, as shown on the right-hand stitch line, the tension on your machine is correct.

YOU WILL NEED

■ Sewing machine
■ 100 per cent cotton sewing thread
■ Fabrics
■ Erasable fabric-marking pen
■ Ruler
■ Straight pins
■ Small, sharp scissors

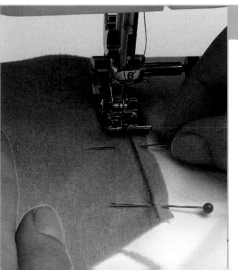

2 Most crazy-patchwork methods specify a seam allowance of 6 mm (¼ in.), whereas project assembly sometimes requires a 9-mm (⅜-in.) or 15-mm (⅝-in.) seam allowance. Most machines have guidelines etched into the throat plate, but when patching, these guidelines are hidden by the backing fabric, so use the presser foot as an approximate 6-mm (¼-in.) guide, matching a straight-cut fabric edge to the right edge of the presser foot or mark a guideline on the patch. Pin the seam securely before you sew.

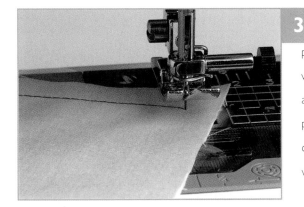

3 When assembling a project (but never for patching), you may need to stitch around a corner. Stop with the needle down at the corner, as shown at left, and lift the presser foot, turn your work, and lower the presser foot to continue in the new direction. On curves, stop every few stitches and reposition your work in the same manner, as required.

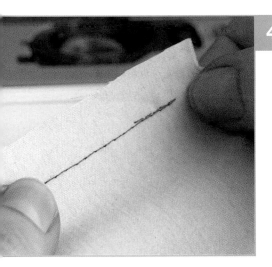

4 When sewing assembly seams, you should secure the thread ends. Begin by stitching about 12 mm (½ in.); then activate the reverse control and stitch back to the beginning of the line. Turn off the reverse control and stitch to the end of the line, removing pins as you come to them. At the end of the line, turn on the reverse control and stitch backwards for about 12 mm (½ in.). Lift the foot and gently pull the work away from the foot for a few inches before cutting the threads close to the fabric.

Zigzag Stitch

This stitch may be used to neaten any raw edges that are liable to fray. It is also useful as a decorative stitch. On most machines, both the stitch width and stitch length can be varied, giving you a wide range of zigzag sizes. The heavier the fabric, the larger the zigzag stitches.

1 Test your machine settings as in Step 1 of Straight Stitch (see opposite). Adjust the thread tension in the same way until the fabric is smooth and the stitches are even (as shown by the right-hand stitch line). You will probably need a slightly looser setting than for straight stitch.

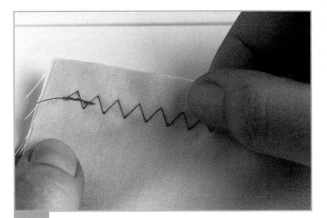

2 If you need to secure the thread tails, begin and end with a few straight stitches, as shown above, reversing in the same manner as for Step 4 of Straight Stitch.

MACHINE EMBROIDERY

Even a basic sewing machine capable only of straight stitch and zigzag stitch can be used to add a variety of decorative stitching to patchwork. More sophisticated sewing machines can often stitch a wide range of embroidered stitch patterns (see page 134); consult your machine's manual and follow the testing and working method below.

Embroidery in a single colour will pull a multicoloured patchwork together, adding a layer of consistency to the design. Conversely, embroidering with several different colours can add variety to a more subtle piece.

1 Make a test sample using the fabrics and assembly method required for the block you want to embroider. The shapes and arrangement can be quite simple. If your project is made by the confetti technique (see page 66), it must be backed with lightweight fabric before embroidery, so your test sample should be backed in the same way. Try a variety of zigzag and other decorative stitches, thread types, and colours, changing the stitch length and width settings as desired. Check the thread tension for each stitch as for ordinary machine sewing (see page 24). Remember that zigzag stitch often requires a slightly looser thread tension than straight stitching. Make a note of the machine settings that work best for each stitch and thread you try.

YOU WILL NEED

- Sewing machine
- Pieced block, with outline marked but not yet trimmed to exact size
- Machine needle appropriate for your fabrics
- Sewing thread
- Machine-embroidery thread
- Spring hoop (optional)
- Erasable fabric-marking pen
- Ruler
- Small, sharp scissors

2 Depending on the weight of your fabrics, you may find it helpful to use an embroidery hoop to prevent the work from puckering. The spring hoop shown here is designed to fit easily under the presser foot, and may be repositioned without removing the work from the machine. Choose stitches and colours appropriate for your project. Stitch along some or all of the seam lines with decorative stitches. You can stitch across a seam line, or to one side of it.

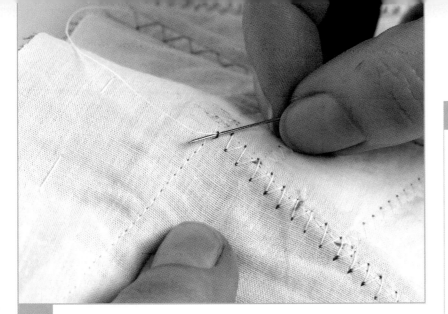

3 As you stitch each line, finish off the thread tails to avoid catching them as you continue stitching. At the outer edges of the block, you can simply snip them off, because the end of the stitched line will be secured when you assemble the project. At the inner end of a stitched line, turn the work over and pull on the bobbin-thread tail to raise a little loop of the upper thread. Use a needle to pull the upper-thread tail through to the back, as shown.

SPECIAL NOTES

■ You can use 100 per cent cotton sewing thread or special machine-embroidery threads, such as metallics, multicoloured threads or glossy viscose rayon thread.

■ As a rule, use ordinary sewing thread in the bobbin, choosing a colour close to the colour of the embroidery thread. If the appearance of the wrong side of your block will be important to the finished project, choose any suitable colour for the bobbin thread and adjust the thread tension correctly for each stitch, as instructed on page 24.

■ If you are embroidering with metallic thread or viscose rayon thread, try the special lightweight polyester bobbin thread appropriate for use with these products.

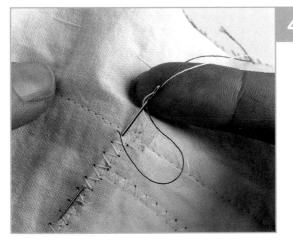

4 Thread a needle with both tails and run them between the layers along the line of stitching, for about 12 mm (½ in.). Snip off the excess thread.

TIPS

■ You can quilt a project with machine embroidery. Make a test sample with the same quilted layers as the project.

■ Some machine-embroidery threads (especially metallics) tend to fray in the needle's eye. To combat this, change to a larger needle size or a special machine embroidery needle and adjust the thread tension carefully; it will probably need to be looser than usual for cotton thread.

5 Continue adding more embroidery until you are happy with your results. You can add interest to plain patches by stitching stripes or checks (draw guidelines first using an erasable fabric-marking pen and ruler), or emphasize a design on a patch by outlining it in a contrasting thread colour. The seams on this block have been embroidered in blue thread, with straight stitch and zigzag stitch, using a variety of stitch lengths and widths.

SEE ALSO

■ Machine Sewing, page 24
■ Machine Embroidery Stitches, page 134

FINISHING

Raw edges that are not enclosed in the seams of a project may be finished in one of two ways. A double hem is suitable only for a single fabric layer, such as the back of the potholder (see page 38) or the lining of the photograph album cover (see page 86). Where the raw edges are made up of several layers as with many crazy-patchwork blocks (with or without quilting), applying bias binding is often the best method of finishing the edges.

SEE ALSO

■ Hand Sewing, page 20
■ Machine Sewing, page 24

Stitching a Double Hem

Use this hem to finish the raw edge of a single layer of fabric. The measurements given may vary according to your project, but the first fold should always be smaller than the second.

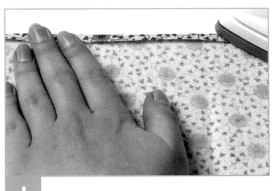

I Fold the raw edge of the fabric 6 mm (¼ in.) to the wrong side of the work and press.

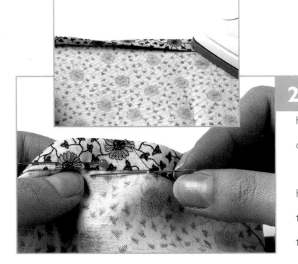

2 Fold the fabric again by a further 9 mm (⅜ in.) and press again. Pin the double hem in place. For slippery or bulky fabrics tack the hem in place using 100 per cent cotton sewing thread that contrasts with the fabric.

Using cotton sewing thread in a colour that blends with the fabric, stitch the hem by hand, using a technique that is similar to slip stitch but that picks up only a tiny amount of fabric (two or three threads) from the single layer of fabric. This way, the stitches are practically invisible on the right side of the work.

3 Alternatively, you can machine-stitch the hem, using cotton sewing thread in a colour that blends with the fabric. Stitch 6 mm (¼ in.) from the outer edge so that the stitches pass through both folds. Remove the tacking stitches.

Applying Bias Binding

Bias binding is made from strips of fabric cut at a 45-degree angle to the straight grain of the fabric, or "on the bias." It is pressed with two sharp folds along the length, which are used as guidelines to stitch it in position. Commercially prepared bias binding is available in cotton, satin, or metallic fabric, and in a wide range of colours and several widths.

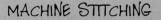

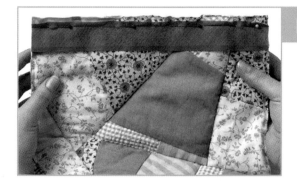

1 Cut a length of bias binding to match the edge that needs binding. Open one of the pressed folds. Pin the binding to the right side of the work, along the open fold, as shown. The distance between the pinned fold and the raw edge should equal half the distance between the two folds of the binding.

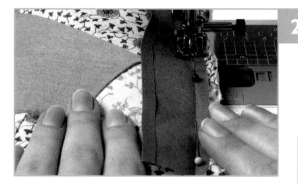

2 Using 100 per cent cotton sewing thread in a colour to match the binding, machine-stitch, as shown, or backstitch exactly along the fold line by hand.

It is possible to machine-stitch the second fold of the bias binding in place, which will save you time, especially when working on large projects. To do this, begin by applying the binding to the *wrong* side of the work, following Steps 1–2 of Applying Bias Binding (left), but *not* working on the front side of the patchwork. When the stitching is complete, fold the binding over to the front side of the work in the same way as in Step 3 (below left), and pin and tack it in place. With the right side up, machine-stitch, very close to the second fold, through all the layers, as shown.

3 Fold the binding over the raw edge so that the second fold meets the stitched line on the wrong side of the work. If you are binding quilted layers, you may need to trim away a little of the wadding. Pin the binding in place or tack, if desired, using cotton thread in a colour that contrasts with the binding. Using cotton thread to match the binding, slip-stitch the second fold in place, as shown, so that it just covers the previous line of stitching. Remove any tacking stitches.

Binding Corners

When it is necessary to bind more than one edge of your work, you will need to bind a neat corner. To apply binding to all four sides of a square or rectangle, first bind two opposite edges as described in Applying Bias Binding (above). Then bind the two remaining edges as follows:

Cut a length of bias binding that is 2.5 cm (1 in.) longer than the raw edge of the work that requires binding. At one end, open the first pressed fold and press 12 mm (½ in.) from the short edge to the wrong side. Repeat with the other end of the binding. Pin the binding in place, as shown.

Machine-sew or backstitch the binding in place by hand, and fold it over the raw edge to meet the stitched line. When you slip-stitch the second fold in place, slip-stitch the corners neatly at the same time.

AFTERCARE

Looking after your crazy-patchwork projects in the ways described here will allow you and your family to enjoy using them for many years to come.

Everyday Protection

The three main causes of damage to needlework, beyond ordinary wear and tear, are daylight, dampness and dirt. Taking a few simple precautions will protect your work from these common problems. Around the home, avoid displaying your work in direct sunlight or close to strong lighting, which may cause the colours to yellow or fade. Whether your work is out on display or stored away in a cupboard, it must be kept dry. In humid conditions avoid storage in plastic bags, and wrap your patchwork in undyed acid-free tissue paper, or keep it in a white cotton bag (or pillowcase). Finally, handwashing is the safest method of cleaning patchwork. Large articles, such as quilts, can be washed by hand in the bath.

Washing Your Patchwork

As long as you have prewashed all of the fabrics and trims in your project, as instructed on page 18, you can wash the completed article gently by hand in the same way.

1 Immerse the crazy patchwork in lukewarm water with a little gentle detergent added. Squeeze the suds gently through the fabric and leave to soak for a few minutes. Do not rub or wring the patchwork.

2 Do not lift the article out of the water; the absorbed water adds extra weight to the patchwork, which can strain the stitches. Instead, while holding the work and gently squeezing it, tilt the basin (or remove the bath plug) to drain the water away, as shown. Rinse three times in cool water, using the same method of letting the water go each time.

3 Blot excess water from the patchwork by rolling it in a clean towel.

CLEANING

■ An article that gets dusty rather than dirty, such as a wall-hanging, will benefit from a gentle shaking every few days. You can also use a vacuum cleaner with an upholstery tool to clean away the dust. Reduce the suction, if possible, and tie a piece of clean muslin over the nozzle to prevent pulling trims or beads into the machine.

■ Before taking a patchwork item to be dry-cleaned, it is a good idea to make a test piece and have that dry-cleaned. Use the same fabrics, embroidery thread, or trims as in your project, particularly if you have included any heirloom fabrics or antique beads or buttons. If you are happy with the results of dry-cleaning the test piece, you can go ahead and have the whole project dry-cleaned. If necessary, beads or buttons, like those shown below, may be removed before dry cleaning.

4 If possible, dry the work flat on another towel. If you need to dry a large article, such as a quilt, place it between two sheets to dry outdoors, away from trees. Press carefully when dry.

ENJOY!

Don't forget, many pieces of patchwork and embroidery have survived for decades (and even centuries) without the benefit of air-conditioning and special detergents. Threads and fabrics will fade in time, but this only adds to the charm of antique pieces. So stitch your project well and look after it as best you can, but never be afraid to have it out on display, where it can be seen and enjoyed by everyone.

Chapter 2

TECHNIQUES AND PROJECTS

Each crazy-patchwork technique (or group of techniques) in this chapter is followed by a project, arranged in order of difficulty. You can begin with the simple colour and composition exercise of making a useful potholder and progress through various methods of assembling and decorating crazy patchwork. Or you can simply dive in, and create whatever inspires you.

COLOUR AND COMPOSITION

YOU WILL NEED

- Fabric scraps
- Fabric scissors
- Cardboard
- Window template (see page 29)
- Paper and pencil, or camera (optional)
- Patchwork equipment, dependent on the patchwork method you have chosen

Sometimes it is difficult to know where to start when choosing fabrics, so before you rush out and buy quantities of different fabrics, it is a good idea to be sure of what you really need. When choosing fabrics for a cushion, take along a scrap of curtain fabric or fabric in the same colour as your sofa. If you are making a bag to coordinate with a special dress, take a fabric sample or the dress with you when you go shopping. Pastel fabrics suit baby gifts; brighter colours are great for an older child's gift.

Choosing Colours

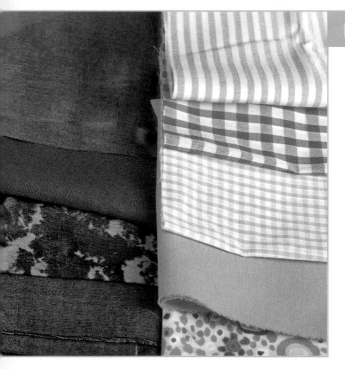

1 Start with scrap fabrics from your stash. Choose colours that might suit your project, but don't worry about fabric types at this stage; even tiny scraps of the wrong sort of fabric can help you decide on colours. Include prints if you wish (see Using Prints, opposite). Decide whether you want all the fabrics to be of a similar value – for example, pastels and medium values – or whether you prefer a mix of light, medium and dark values, as shown. For most crazy patchwork, except the confetti technique (see page 66), you will need at least six or seven fabrics, although you can use as many more as you like. Arrange the fabrics on a flat surface, folding them loosely to the same size as shown at left. Stand back and take a good look to determine whether any one piece jumps out at you because it is too light or too dark. If so, either remove it or balance it with another similar fabric. If a fabric is just plain "wrong," like the green/blue splashy print shown in the photo, take it away. Notice textures, too: The glossy jade satin adds variety but is more difficult to care for.

SEE ALSO

- Fabric Preparation, page 18
- Blocks and Templates, page 28
- The Fabric Collection, page 138

2 Make sure all of the fabrics you have chosen are of similar weight and are suitable for your project (see the Fabric Collection, page 138). If not, you can shop for replacements, knowing what to look for. To make a shopping card, cut little snippets of all of the fabrics, both the ones to use and the ones to replace or buy more of, and put an asterisk by any other colours you would like to include. Patterned snippets should be large enough to include all the colours on the print. Make sure the fabrics you buy are of a suitable fibre content and weight.

Building a Composition

Most crazy-patchwork techniques have resulted from people working by instinct, trying things out as they go rather than having a definite plan. Sometimes it's difficult to get started, so try these ideas.

1 Fold your chosen scraps into three- and four-sided shapes and arrange them together, roughly into the size of the block you are making. Overlap them to represent the size of the patches you want. Move them around and try different arrangements, viewing them through a window template (see page 29), as shown. Decide which fabrics look good next to each other and which should be separated. You can make a sketch (or take a photograph) to guide you as you cut and place the patches.

2 Be flexible. You can change your mind about a colour or shape at any stage. When you are about three-quarters of the way through piecing a block, put your work to one side and take a break. Come back later and look carefully to check the balance of the colours and shapes. You can make any adjustments you like at this stage.

TIPS

■ When choosing colours, leave your fabric selection displayed while you take a break. Then walk back into the room and take another look. Do the fabrics still work together? Is there another colour you'd like to see included?

■ Begin by sewing a patch from each fabric in turn; then use them all again to piece further patches in a different order.

■ Adding embroidery and/or trims can also help to balance or unify a composition.

■ If you want to plan a block exactly (for example, to make several identical blocks), use the technique described for paper-template piecing (see page 90).

Using Prints

As a rule, be cautious when using busy prints. Simple patterns, stripes, and checks are easier to work with than more detailed prints. Small-scale patterns or splashy, blurry prints are generally easier to use than patterns with large, well-defined motifs.

Blending Fabrics

Choose two (or more) patterned fabrics, such as this multicoloured print and the striped fabric; add plain fabrics in matching and contrasting colours and textures.

Selecting an Area

Sometimes a small scrap cut from a large-scale print can provide just the touch of colour you need. This leaf, in two shades of green, can be used for its colour alone; when used as a small patch, it will no longer be identifiable as a leaf.

POTHOLDER

This cheerful potholder makes an ideal gift for the chef in your family and will look great hanging in the kitchen or next to the grill. The patching technique used for this project is very simple, so you may want to make several! Six bright colours are used here, but you can choose any colour combination you like.

YOU WILL NEED

- Sewing equipment: erasable fabric-marking pen; ruler; dressmaker's shears; pinking shears; paper scissors; small, sharp scissors; straight pins; hand-sewing needle; sewing machine; iron
- Window or plastic template, 20 x 20 cm (8 x 8 in.)
- Lightweight cotton backing fabric, 25 x 50 cm (10 x 20 in.)
- Felt fabric scraps in six colours, each approximately 10 x 15 cm (4 x 6 in.)
- 100 per cent cotton sewing thread to match bias binding
- 100 per cent cotton sewing thread to match the lining fabric
- Lightweight cotton lining fabric, 25 x 50 cm (10 x 20 in.)
- Compressed fleece wadding, 25 x 50 cm (10 x 20 in.)
- Bias binding, 1 m x 2.5 cm (40 in. x 1 in.)
- Ribbon, 10 cm x 12 mm (4 in. x ½ in.)

FINISHED SIZE

- 20 x 20 cm (8 x 8 in.)

1 Use an erasable fabric-marking pen and the window template to draw an 20 x 20-cm (8 x 8-in.) square onto one end of a 25 x 50-cm (10 x 20-in.) piece of lightweight cotton backing fabric. Cut out the square, staying at least 12 mm (½ in.) outside the marked line. Use pinking shears to cut out a felt rectangle of roughly 5 x 7.5 cm (2 x 3 in.) and pin it to one corner of the backing fabric, overlapping the marked outline by 6 mm (¼ in.), as shown.

2 Cut another felt rectangle and pin it next to the first rectangle, overlapping it and the marked outline on the backing fabric by 6 mm (¼ in.). Set your sewing machine to a medium-length wide zigzag stitch and stitch along the overlap, using 100 per cent cotton sewing thread in a colour that matches the bias binding (to be used later). Trim the ends of the threads, as shown.

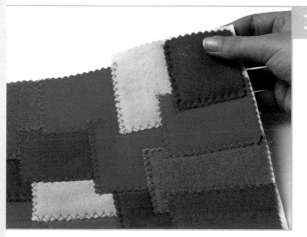

3 Working towards the opposite corner, pin and stitch more rectangles of felt to the backing fabric, always overlapping previous pieces and the outline on the backing fabric by at least 6 mm (¼ in.). Some pieces will need to be stitched on two or three sides. Continue until the patches completely cover the marked square on the backing fabric.

4 Stitch two or three straight lines of zigzag stitch across the patchwork in each direction to form a grid. Use the window template and erasable fabric-marking pen to redraw the outline of the square on the right side of the patchwork. Using a thread that blends with the lining fabric (to be used later), zigzag-stitch just inside the marked outline, all around the outside edge of the patchwork block. Cut out the block along the marked outline, as shown.

TIP

Before sewing the felt pieces to the backing fabric, test the thread tension on your sewing machine on several scraps of the same layers of fabric, as shown on page 25.

SEE ALSO

■ Hand Sewing, page 20
■ Machine Sewing, page 24
■ Finishing, page 30

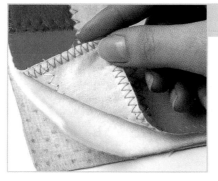

5 Cut out an 20 × 20-cm (8 × 8-in.) square of lightweight cotton lining fabric and another from the wadding. Lay the lining fabric square on your work surface, right side down. Place the square of wadding on top of the lining fabric and lay the patchwork block, right side up, on top of the wadding, as shown. Pin and sew tacking stitches by hand through all of the layers, all around the outside edge, about 3 mm (⅛ in.) in from the raw edges.

6 Use a photocopier to enlarge the hand-pocket template from page 152 by the percentage given. Cut out the template and use it to cut one shape from backing fabric, one from lining fabric, and one from wadding. Layer the shapes on top of one another in the same way as in Step 5, with the backing fabric replacing the patchwork block. Pin and sew tacking stitches about 3 mm (⅛ in.) in from the edges to secure the layers together. Stitch bias binding to the diagonal edge, following the instructions on page 31. Trim the binding to match the edges of the pocket, as shown.

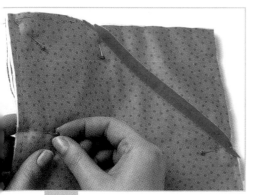

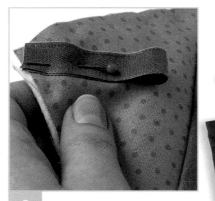

7 Place the patchwork piece and the pocket piece together, with the lining uppermost on the pocket piece. Pin through all the layers, as shown, and sew tacking stitches around the edge again.

8 Fold a length of ribbon in half to form a loop and pin to the top corner of the potholder. Sew bias binding to all four sides of the potholder, treating the corners as shown on page 31.

SEW-AND-FLIP

This machine-stitching method can seem rather confusing at first, but with a little practice it is easy to work. Here, a selection of lightweight plain and printed cottons is featured, with the addition of gingham check to make a block suitable for a quilt. Medium-weight fabrics, such as cottons, silk dupion or dress-weight velvets, would make a block suitable for a cushion or tote bag.

YOU WILL NEED

- Window or plastic template (see page 29)
- Erasable fabric-marking pen
- Backing fabric, at least 2.5 cm (1 in.) larger all around than block
- Fabrics: At least six, in similar weights (light- or medium-weight)
- Large fabric scissors and small, sharp scissors
- Pins
- 100 per cent cotton sewing thread
- Sewing machine
- Iron
- Sewing needle

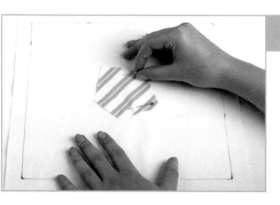

1 Use an erasable fabric-marking pen and a window or plastic template to mark the size of the block on the backing fabric. Cut a four- or five-sided patch and pin it somewhere near the centre, right side up, as shown.

2 Cut another patch, such as this irregular shape, and pin it right side down onto the first patch, matching two straight edges, as shown.

3 All seams are stitched in the following way: Machine-stitch, leaving a seam allowance of 6 mm (¼ in.), as shown. Stitch only where there are three layers of fabric (two patches plus the backing fabric), and leave 6 mm (¼ in.) unstitched at each end of the seam. There is no need to secure the thread ends with reverse stitching; just snip them off.

4 Press along the stitched line to smooth the stitches and flip the second patch over, right side up, as shown.

5 Press the seam flat, using an iron, as shown. Smooth the new patch away from the seam.

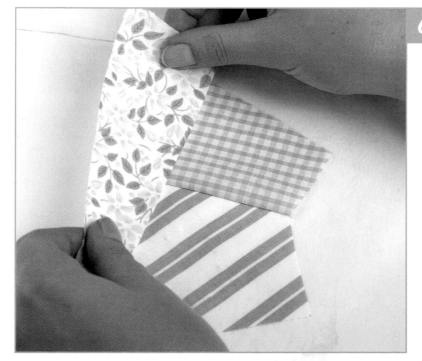

6 Patches can be triangular or four-sided, irregular rectangles. To try the effect of the next patch, press 6 mm (¼ in.) to the wrong side along one edge and place it anywhere you like on your work, overlapping both previous patches by at least 6 mm (¼ in.).

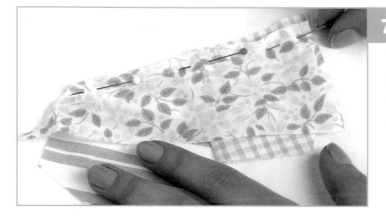

7 Flip the patch, wrong side up, and pin it in place, as shown. Stitch along the fold line, remembering that the seam allowance should always be 6 mm (¼ in.). All of the seams should be straight, with no curves; otherwise, the finished patchwork will not lie flat.

8 Trim the edges of the first and second patches to match the seam allowance on the third patch, as shown. This will keep the patchwork surface smooth and prevent excess bulk. Save any scraps that can be used elsewhere. You may need to unpick a few stitches of a previous seam. Make sure to remove all thread ends; otherwise, they will get caught between the layers.

9 Continue adding patches as in Steps 6–8, making sure that there are no little gaps between the pieces. As you proceed, you will find that you need longer and longer patches: To avoid this effect, join two or three smaller pieces together and press the seams to one side, as shown. You can use the ruler and fabric-marking erasable pen to draw a straight line along one edge of such a piece, as shown, and then stitch it down, as before.

10 Sometimes a piece needs to be stitched down along more than one edge, which is not possible by machine. Press the seam allowance to the wrong side along the required edges as shown, and sew one edge by machine.

11 Flip and press this patch as before and pin the unattached edge(s) in place, as shown, tucking the corners underneath neatly. If necessary, reduce bulk by snipping notches at the corners. You can then slip-stitch these edges by hand (see page 21) or tack them in place and attach them later with embroidery.

TIPS

■ You can use as many different fabrics as you like. If you have a limited number (six or seven), try to use each fabric two or three times.

■ If you are making several blocks for a quilt, try beginning each block with a different fabric and vary the order in whlch you add the remaining fabrics.

12 Around the edges, patches should completely overlap the marked block outline, with no gaps. Use the template to redraw the block outline, as shown. You can change the position slightly if you wish.

13 Tack by hand just inside the newly marked block outlines, as shown. Your block is now ready for embroidery or quilting, or for assembly into a project.

SEE ALSO:
■ Blocks and Templates, page 28
■ Machine Sewing, page 24
■ Hand Sewing, page 20

DRAWSTRING BAG

You can make your own version of this useful bag using your favourite colours and prints, with or without the embroidery. Lightweight cotton fabrics are particularly suitable; here we have used solid colours, gingham checks, and two prints, all in shades of blue, turquoise, and white. The sew-and-flip technique is used, and simple hand embroidery is worked along the patchwork seams. Other suitable techniques for this bag include hand piecing (see page 48), strip piecing (see page 54), the fusible-web method (see page 60), and the confetti technique (see page 66). You could also substitute machine embroidery for the hand embroidery (see page 26).

1 Photocopy the drawstring-bag base template from page 152, enlarging by the percentage given. Check that the radius line on the circle measures exactly 10 cm (4 in.), then cut out the template. Using your preferred patching technique, make two crazy-patchwork blocks – one large enough to cover the circular base template and the other to form a 31 x 59.5-cm (12 ¼ x 23 ½-in.) rectangle. Redraw the outlines of the circular and rectangular patchwork blocks, using an erasable fabric-marking pen, then sew tacking stitches all around the shapes, just inside the marked lines. Cut out the blocks along the marked outlines. Cut out two pieces of lightweight cotton lining fabric to match the patchwork blocks.

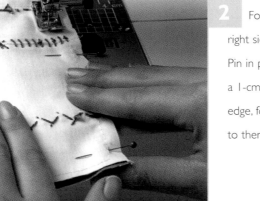

2 Fold the patchwork rectangle in half, with right sides together, matching the two short sides. Pin in place and machine-stitch or backstitch with a 1-cm (⅜-in.) seam allowance along the short edge, forming a tube. Remove pins as you come to them. Press the seam open.

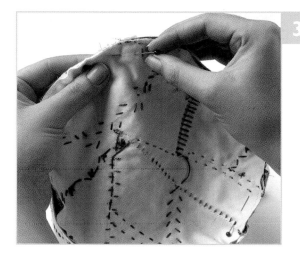

3 With wrong sides facing you, pin the patchwork base circle to the tube, with right sides together, as shown. If the circle seems too large, increase the seam allowance slightly from 1 cm (⅜ in.). If the circle is too small, decrease the seam allowance. Sew tacking stitches by hand all around on the seam line to ensure an accurate fit.

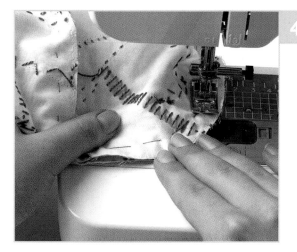

4 With the wrong side of the bag base on top, machine-stitch the base circle to the main part of the bag or backstitch it by hand. For extra strength and to secure the ends of any embroidery thread that have been cut, stitch around the bag base twice. Remove the tacking stitches.

SEE ALSO

- Sew-and-Flip, page 40
- Hand Sewing, page 20
- Machine Sewing, page 24
- Hand Embroidery, page 22
- The Stitch Collection, page 106
- Finishing, page 30
- Ribbons and Trims, page 80

5 Snip wide notches into the seam allowance all around the bag base, at 2-cm (¾-in.) intervals. Press the seam allowance open.

6 Assemble the lining by following Steps 2–4, using the lining-fabric shapes from Step 1.

7 Turn the outer bag right side out and slip the lining piece inside it, with wrong sides together, and match the seams. Pin the two layers together all around the top edge, and sew tacking stitches through both layers 3 mm (⅛ in.) below the raw edge, as shown.

8 To bind the top edge, open one end of the satin binding and fold it diagonally. Press firmly. Pin this end across the centre seam on the outside of the bag.

9 Pin the binding all around the top edge of the bag, overlapping the folded end completely.

10 Arrange the ends of the binding as shown, and machine-stitch the binding in place or backstitch along the crease of the binding by hand.

11 Fold the binding to the inside of the bag and slip-stitch it in place. Also slip-stitch along the diagonal fold where it overlaps the end of the binding.

12 Using a ruler and erasable fabric-marking pen, mark positions for ten eyelets, all 5 cm (2 in.) down from the top edge of the bag, as follows: one eyelet 2.9 cm (1 ⅛ in.) on either side of the centre seam, and eight more eyelets evenly spaced at intervals of about 5.75 cm (2 ¼ in.).

13 Apply the eyelets following the manufacturer's instructions and using the tools supplied in the eyelet kit. Beginning at an eyelet to one side of the centre back seam, thread strong rayon cord all around, in and out of the eyelets.

14 Tie the two ends of the rayon cord with an overhand knot, leaving tails of about 7.5 cm (3 in.). Fray the tails to form a tassel.

TIPS

■ If any of your marked eyelet positions fall on hand-embroidered seams, simply snip the embroidery thread and unpick a few of the embroidery stitches. Run the thread tails into the fabric, away from the eyelet position before cutting the eyelet hole.

■ For extra security, paint the eyelet position with Fraycheck or fabric glue before cutting the eyelet.

■ After fraying the cord ends to form the tassel, wet the tassel to remove any kinks and, when dry, press it with a moderately hot iron.

NEEDLE CASE AND SCISSORS HOLDER

- Sewing equipment: erasable fabric-marking pen; tape measure; ruler; dressmaker's shears; pinking shears; small, sharp scissors; straight pins; hand-sewing needle; sewing machine; iron
- 6 lightweight cotton, silk, and medium-weight velvet fabric scraps, approximately 15 x 15 cm (6 x 6 in.) each
- Lightweight cotton backing fabric, 20 x 15 cm (8 x 6 in.)
- 100 per cent cotton sewing thread to contrast with fabrics for tacking stitches
- 100 per cent cotton sewing thread to blend with fabrics for final stitching
- Embroidery thread in desired colour
- Embroidery needle to suit the thread used (see table, page 23)
- Lightweight cotton lining fabric, 15 x 10 cm (6 x 4 in.)
- Lightweight wadding, 5 x 10 cm (6 x 4 in.)
- Thin twisted cord or narrow ribbon, 7.5 cm (3 in.) long
- Bias binding, 61 cm (24 in.) long and 12.5 cm (½ in.) wide
- Two pieces of felt, each 8 x 13 cm (3¼ x 5¼ in.), in desired colour
- Button

FINISHED SIZE
- 7.5 x 10 cm (3 x 4 in.)

These little projects are so quick and so much fun to make, they're ideal for trying out different piecing methods. Here we have used the hand-piecing technique with two cotton batik prints, solid-coloured silks, and lightweight velvet that echoes the colours of the prints, and then added hand embroidery. However, you can make the crazy patchwork using your favourite patching method and your choice of lightweight fabrics.

Needle Case

1 Mark a 15 x 10-cm (6 x 4-in.) rectangle on an 20 x 15-cm (8 x 6-in.) piece of lightweight cotton backing fabric. Using any of the piecing techniques featured in this book, make a crazy-patchwork block that covers the marked outline. Add some hand-embroidery stitches to the patchwork seams, if desired. The block shown here was made by hand piecing and embroidered with pink cotton embroidery thread. Using an erasable fabric-marking pen, redraw the outline of the 15 x 10-cm (6 x 4-in.) rectangle on the front side of the patchwork, and sew tacking stitches all around the outside edges of the block, just *inside* the marked line. Cut out the block along the marked outline, as shown.

2 Place the 15 x 10-cm (6 x 4-in.) rectangle of lightweight cotton lining fabric right side down on a flat surface. Position the 15 x 10-cm (6 x 4-in.) rectangle of lightweight wadding on top of the lining fabric and place the patchwork block on top of the wadding, right side up. Pin through all of the layers and sew tacking stitches all around, 3 mm (⅛ in.) in from the outside edges, as shown.

3 Fold a 7.5-cm (3-in.) length of twisted cord or 3-mm (⅛-in.) wide ribbon in half. Pin the loop to the centre of one side edge, as shown, and use a few tacking stitches to secure it. The loop will be on the back of the finished needle case, and the tacking stitches will be covered by bias binding.

4 Apply bias binding to all four edges beginning with the long sides, following the instructions on page 31.

5 Use pinking shears to trim the edges of the two pieces of felt for the pages of the needle case.

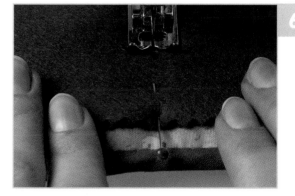

6 Fold the patchwork cover in half to find the centre, and mark the fold line on the inside with the erasable fabric-marking pen. Match the centre of the felt pages to this line and pin them in place. Using the blending cotton sewing thread, machine-stitch through all thicknesses, as shown.

7 Sew a button to the front of the case at the centre of the short side, just inside the bound edge. The cord loop attached in Step 3 to the back edge should fit neatly over the button.

SEE ALSO
- Hand Piecing, page 48
- Hand Sewing, page 20
- Machine Sewing, page 24
- Hand Embroidery, page 22
- The Stitch Collection, page 106
- Finishing, page 30
- Blocks and Templates, page 28

Scissors Holder

1 Photocopy the template on page 153, enlarging by the percentage given. Cut out the paper template and draw around it onto template plastic or cardboard and cut out the shape. Draw around the template onto the backing fabric. Using your preferred piecing technique, make a patchwork block to cover the outline of the template. Add some hand-embroidery stitches to the patchwork seams, if desired. Using an erasable fabric-marking pen, redraw the template outline on the right side of the patchwork block and sew tacking stitches all around, just inside the marked line, as shown. Cut out the patchwork block along the marked outline.

2 Cut out the lightweight cotton lining fabric and lightweight wadding to match the shape of the cutout block. Place the lining fabric right side down on a flat surface. Position the wadding on top of the lining fabric and the patchwork on top of the wadding, right side up. Pin and tack all around, through all layers, 3 mm (⅛ in.) in from the outside edges, as shown.

3 Apply bias binding to the curved edge following the instructions on page 31.

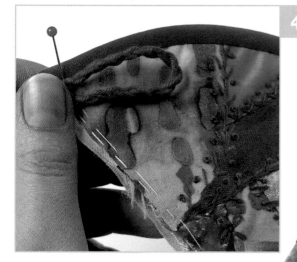

4 Fold a 7.5-cm (3-in.) length of thin twisted cord or narrow ribbon in half. Pin the loop to the top corner, as shown, and use a few tacking stitches to secure it.

5 Fold the work in half, with wrong sides together, matching the straight edges. Apply bias binding to the straight edge, as shown, folding in the raw ends as described on page 31 and catching the loop into the seam. Stitch the corners neatly.

STRIP PIECING

This simple machine-stitching technique requires narrow strips of fabric to be stitched down across the width of the block. It is good for using up remnants, and it is also suitable for large blocks and for heavier fabrics.

YOU WILL NEED

- Window or plastic template (see page 29)
- Erasable fabric-marking pen
- Backing fabric, at least 2.5 cm (1 in.) larger all around than block
- Fabrics in similar weights (light- or medium-weight)
- Fabric scissors and small, sharp scissors
- Straight pins
- 100 per cent cotton sewing thread
- Sewing machine
- Iron
- Sewing needle for tacking

1 Using an erasable fabric-marking pen and a window or plastic template, draw the block size you require on the backing fabric. Cut tapering strips of fabric, as shown, about 2.5 cm (1 in.) longer than the width of the block, using the ruler. Strips can taper from about 5–7.5 cm (2–3 in.) down to 2.5–5 cm (1–2 in.), or you can cut them wider for a larger project.

2 Place the first strip, right side up, at one end of the block, overlapping the block outline by at least 6 mm (¼ in.).

3 Place the second strip, right side down on top of the first, with two long edges together inside the block, as shown. The edges don't have to match exactly; you can set the second strip at a slight angle if you prefer. Pin through all the layers, as shown. If necessary, use the ruler and fabric-marking pen to draw a straight stitching line with a seam allowance of 6 mm (¼ in.).

4 Stitch the seam by hand or machine, beginning and ending 6 mm (¼ in.) outside the marked outline. The seam must be straight. If necessary, trim the edge of the first strip to match the second, as shown, so it cannot show through as a dark "shadow."

5 Press along the stitching line to "set" the stitches. Then flip the second strip over, right side up, and press, as shown.

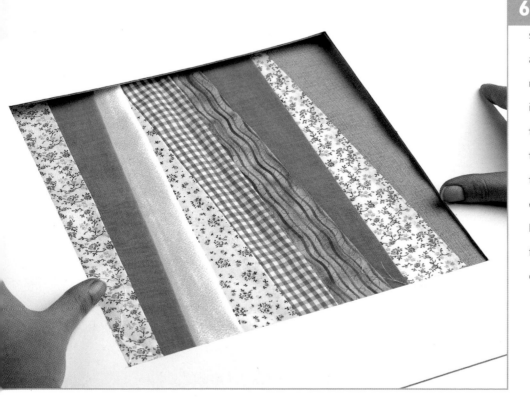

6 Continue adding more strips in the same way, alternating the wide and narrow ends until the block is covered. Use the window template, as shown, to mark the outline of the block and tack all around the outside edge, just inside the marked line. The block is now ready for quilting, embroidery, or assembly.

Diagonal Variation

1 Begin with a diagonal strip across the centre of the block, as shown. Add the next strip at one side, following Steps 3–5 on page 54.

2 Continue adding strips, roughly on the diagonal, across to one corner. All strips should overlap the block outline by at least 6 mm (¼ in.). End with a triangular patch, as shown.

3 To complete the block, work from the centre outwards to the opposite corner. Redraw the block outline, using the window or plastic template and erasable fabric-marking pen and tack all around, as usual.

Triangle Variation

1 Divide the backing fabric block with a diagonal line, making two triangles. You can also divide your fabrics into two colour groups, using one group to cover each triangular half of the block. Follow Steps 3–5 on page 54, to cover one triangle with strips at right angles to the diagonal line, working outwards from the centre to one corner and then the other. End all of the seam lines just one stitch over the marked diagonal line.

2 Cover the other triangle with strips from the second colour group, placing and sewing roughly parallel to the diagonal line and working from the centre outwards to the corner.

3 Redraw the block outline using the window template and tack around the outside edge, as usual.

TIPS

■ All seams must be perfectly straight; otherwise, the completed block will not lie flat.

■ If you prefer to stitch by hand, you can backstitch the seams instead of machine stitching them

SEE ALSO

■ Blocks and Templates, page 28
■ Hand Sewing, page 20
■ Machine Sewing, page 24

TOTE BAG

This pretty bag can be used to hold your needlework in progress, or as a useful carry-all. The crazy-patchwork block shown here has been made using the strip-piecing technique and a selection of medium-weight cotton and silk fabrics. While you could choose any other piecing technique, it is not advisable to use heavyweight fabrics or fusible web for this project, because the top edge of the bag will be too bulky to form neat folds. To vary the design, you could add hand or machine embroidery, beads or sequins.

YOU WILL NEED

- Sewing equipment: erasable fabric-marking pen; ruler; dressmaker's shears; small, sharp scissors; straight pins; hand-sewing needle; sewing machine; iron
- 8 medium-weight cotton and silk fabric scraps approximately 45 x 15 cm (18 x 16 in.) each
- Lightweight cotton backing fabric, 43 x 73.5 cm (17 x 29 in.)
- 100 per cent cotton sewing thread to contrast with fabrics for tacking stitches
- 100 per cent cotton sewing thread to blend with fabrics for final stitching
- Lightweight cotton lining fabric, 40 x 71 cm (16 x 28 in.)
- Blunt knitting needle or point turner
- Two wooden rings, each 12.5 cm (5 in.) in diameter

FINISHED SIZE

- Approximately 38 x 33 cm (15 x 13 in.)

1 Choose wooden rings that look well with your fabrics. Mark a 40 x 71-cm (16 x 28-in.) rectangle on the 43 x 73.5-cm (17 x 29-in.) piece of cotton backing fabric. Using any piecing technique *except* the fusible-web method, make a patchwork block to cover the marked outline. Redraw the outline onto the right side of the patchwork; tack all around it, just inside the marked outline. Cut out the rectangular block along the marked outline. Cut out a rectangle of lightweight cotton lining fabric to match the size of the cut patchwork block.

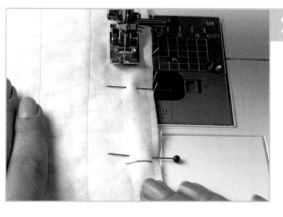

2 Fold the patchwork in half with right sides together, matching the short edges. Measure 20 cm (8 in.) up from the fold and make a mark at this point on each side edge. Pin along each side from the marked point down to the fold. With a seam allowance of 12 mm (½ in.), backstitch by hand or machine-sew the side seams, using cotton sewing thread that blends with the patchwork fabrics.

3 Snip diagonally across the two lower corners, close to the end of the stitched lines, making sure that the scissors do not cut through the stitching. Press the seam allowances open.

4 Repeat Steps 2–3 with the lining fabric from Step 1, leaving it inside out.

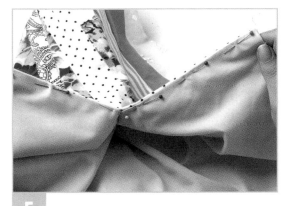

5 Turn the patchwork bag right side out, pushing out the corners neatly, using a blunt knitting needle or point turner. Press the patchwork; then slip the lining bag inside the outer patchwork bag, aligning the side seams. Match the unseamed side edges of the lining and the outer bag and pin them together, as shown. Working from inside the bag and using cotton sewing thread that blends with the fabrics, slip-stitch the lining to the outer bag on each side by hand.

SEE ALSO
- Strip Piecing, page 54
- Hand Sewing, page 20
- Machine Sewing, page 24

6 At the top edges of the bag, fold the patchwork and lining over by 12 mm (½ in.) to the wrong side. Press both layers together and pin and tack both edges, as shown.

7 Fold one of the top edges again by another 2.5 cm (1 in.) and press. Slip a wooden ring beneath this second fold and pin the top edge over the ring, as shown. Use blending thread to slip-stitch along the folded edge, holding the ring in place. Begin and end this stitching very securely. Pin and stitch the other ring to the opposite top edge in the same way.

FUSIBLE WEB

YOU WILL NEED

For a 25-cm (10-in.) block, you will need:

- Fabrics in similar weights (light- or medium-weight)
- Pencil
- Ruler
- Fusible web, approximately 46 x 46 cm (18 x 18 in.)
- Iron
- Paper and fabric scissors
- Straight pins
- Backing fabric, 30 x 30 cm (12 x 12 in.), plus extra scrap for test sample
- Window or plastic template (see page 29)
- Erasable fabric-marking pen
- Damp press cloth
- Embroidery equipment (see page 10)

Fusible web is made from fibre that melts when heated, which allows you to permanently fuse two layers of fabric together with a hot iron. It is normally supplied on a paper backing. For best results always follow the fusing instructions provided with the specific product you purchase.

Fusing crazy patches onto backing fabric creates a firm, strong fabric suitable for tote bags, pillows and furnishings. The edges of the patches are not turned under, so you can use fairly heavy fabrics, such as canvas or velvet, but all fabrics must be able to withstand the heat of the ironing process.

1 Make a test sample using the exact fabrics you intend to use for the block. Draw small shapes on the paper side of the fusible web in pencil. Use paper scissors to cut between the shapes to separate them, as shown, but do not cut the shapes out accurately yet.

2 Iron each shape onto the wrong side of a scrap of each patchwork fabric with a medium iron, or follow the manufacturer's instructions. Use fabric scissors to cut out the shapes accurately along the marked outlines as shown at left. Use a pin to peel the backing paper from each piece, as shown at right.

3 Fuse the pieces to a piece of backing fabric, overlapping the edges by 3 mm (⅛ in.). Some lightweight fabrics may bond better with no steam. Discard any fabrics that wrinkle, change their appearance, or do not bond successfully.

4 Now you are ready to make your block. Use a window or plastic template and an erasable fabric-marking pen to draw the block outline on the backing fabric, as shown. For the first patch, begin at one corner. Lay the fusible web paper-side-down on the block and use the fabric-marking pen to draw the outline of the patch you want, overlapping the outer edge of the block by about 12 mm (½ in.).

5 Using the paper scissors, cut out the fusible-web shape, about 6 mm (¼ in.) outside the drawn outline, and iron it to the wrong side of your chosen fabric. Use the fabric scissors to cut out the patch accurately along the drawn outline, as shown.

6 Peel off the backing paper, place the patch right side up where required on the block, and use the tip of a warm iron to "tack" it in place at the centre, as shown, using just enough pressure to slightly melt the web so that the patch will not move. Patches "tacked" in this way can be lifted and replaced if necessary.

7 For the next patch, lay the fusible web paper-side-down over the block and trace the outline with the fabric-marking pen, adding an overlap of 3 mm (⅛ in.) where this patch meets the previous one. Repeat Steps 5–6. Continue adding patches, as shown, until the block is completely covered. You can now arrange the overlaps and snip off any unwanted corners. All of the pieces should overlap by 3 mm (⅛ in.). When you are satisfied with the arrangement, fuse the patches in place as instructed by the manufacturer. This usually requires a damp pressing cloth and a medium-hot iron. Allow the block to dry flat for about 20 minutes and set completely. Then use the template to redraw the block outline.

TIPS

■ If you wish, you can plan your block by drawing the shapes you want on the backing fabric. Or you can proceed by instinct and make up the pattern as you go along.

■ Use a ruler to draw straight lines. For curves, use a pair of compasses or draw around a cup, saucer, or plate.

SEE ALSO

■ Blocks and Templates, page 28
■ Hand Embroidery, page 22
■ Machine Embroidery, page 26

Cover all of the raw fabric edges with embroidery. Even though the edges are fused in place, with wear and tear, they may begin to fray. This block has been machine-embroidered with a variety of stitches. If you prefer, you can embroider by hand with stitches close together.

EVENING PURSE

Choose exotic fabrics such as silks, velvets and brocades to make this glamorous purse. Fabrics like these can be difficult to handle, so use the fusible-web technique on page 60 for the patchwork. Here, machine embroidery in metallic gold and glossy rayon threads is featured.

YOU WILL NEED

- Sewing equipment: erasable fabric-marking pen; ruler; dressmaker's shears; small, sharp scissors; paper scissors; straight pins; hand-sewing needle; sewing machine; iron
- 10 silk, velvet and brocade fabric scraps, approximately 20 x 20 cm (8 x 8 in.) each
- Lightweight cotton backing fabric, 30 x 53 cm (12 x 21 in.)
- Lightweight cotton or silk lining fabric, 25 x 48 cm (10 x 19 in.)
- Fusible web, approximately 60 x 45 cm (24 x 18 in.)
- 100 per cent cotton sewing thread to contrast with fabrics for tacking stitches
- Decorative machine-embroidery thread in desired colours
- 100 per cent cotton sewing thread to blend with the fabrics for final stitching
- 3 mm (⅛ in.)-wide ribbon, 61 cm (24 in.) long
- Rayon cord, 2 m (80 in.) long
- Blunt knitting needle or point turner
- Embroidery thread in desired colours for binding handle
- Fraycheck or fabric glue
- Beads in desired sizes

FINISHED SIZE

- 23 x 23 cm (9 x 9 in.)

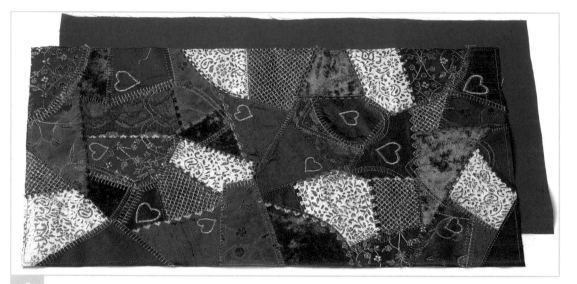

1 Mark a 25 x 48-cm (10 x 19-in.) rectangle on the 30 x 53-cm (12 x 21-in.) piece of lightweight cotton backing fabric. Using the fusible-web patching technique on page 60, make a crazy-patchwork block to cover the marked outline. (Use the paper scissors to cut out the fusible web before pressing it to the fabric scraps.) Use an erasable fabric-marking pen to redraw the outline of the rectangle on the right side of the completed patchwork block. Use a contrasting cotton sewing thread to sew tacking stitches (or do zigzag stitch on a sewing machine), all around the edges of the patchwork block, just inside the marked outline. Cut out the patchwork along the marked outline to match the size of the lining, as shown.

2 Add machine embroidery using decorative threads, such as metallic gold or glossy rayon. Here, heart outlines of various sizes have been embroidered.

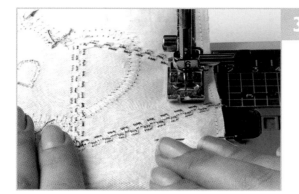

3 Fold the patchwork block in half, with right sides together, matching the short sides. Pin and machine-sew the side seams or backstitch them by hand, leaving a seam allowance of 12 mm (½ in.).

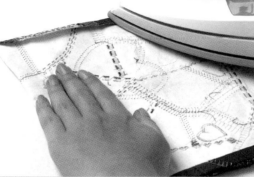

4 Snip diagonally across the lower corners at the fold, close to the stitching.

5 Press the seam allowances open on both sides.

SEE ALSO

■ Fusible-web, page 60
■ Hand Sewing, page 20
■ Machine Sewing, page 24
■ Machine Embroidery, page 26
■ Machine-embroidery Stitches, page 134
■ Finishing, page 30

6 All around the top edge, fold 12 mm (½ in.) to the wrong side and press.

7 Cut the 61-cm (24-in.) length of 3-mm (⅛-in.)-wide ribbon in half. Pin one end of one half at centre front of the top edge, and one end of the other half at centre back. Stitch the ends in place to the seam allowance only, as shown.

8 Unfold the top edge. Cut the 2-m (80-in.) length of rayon cord in half. Line the two cords up side by side, then pin two ends to the seam allowance at one side seam, as shown. Machine-sew across the cord two or three times to secure it firmly. Attach the other ends of the cords to the opposite-side seam in the same way.

9 Turn the purse right side out, pushing out the corners as neatly as possible using a blunt knitting needle or a point turner. Fold the top edge back inside and press. Catch the ends of the cords to the side seams with hand stitching, without stitching through to the right side of the purse. Make up the lining following Steps 3–6 with the lining fabric from Step 1, leaving the lining wrong side out. Slip the lining inside the purse, matching the seams, and pin all around. Slip-stitch the folded edge of the lining just below the folded edge of the purse, covering the ends of the cords and ribbons, as shown.

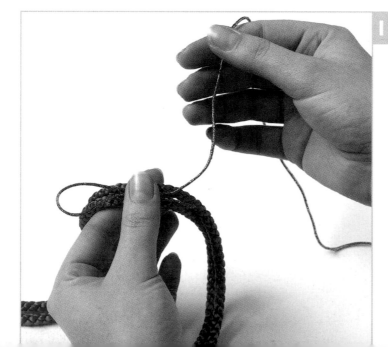

10 Embroidery thread is used to bind the two cords together at intervals of about 12.5 cm (5 in.). Cut a 1-m (40-in.) length of thread for each binding. Take one length of thread and make a loop of about 7.5 cm (3 in.) at one end. Lay the loop along the cords, as shown.

11 Bind the free end tightly around the cords, toward the loop, for about 2.5 cm (1 in.), then pass the free end of thread through the loop, as shown.

12 Pull gently on the starting tail to bring the loop and the free end under the binding. Snip off the tails and paint the binding with a little Fraycheck or fabric glue. Repeat steps 10–12 at desired intervals.

13 Thread a needle onto a ribbon end and use it to thread on beads in an arrangement of your choice. When you are happy with the arrangement, unthread the needle and knot the ribbon end to keep the beads in place. Repeat with the second ribbon.

CONFETTI

This is a quick and easy machine-stitching method that is worked without a backing fabric. The fabrics should be lightweight; otherwise, the seams will become very bulky. Start with fairly large pieces. Only a few different fabrics are required, so choose a mix of plain, printed and gingham cottons for variety.

YOU WILL NEED

For a 25-cm (10-in.) block you will need:

- Lightweight fabrics: four pieces approximately 30 x 15 cm (12 x 6 in.) and a fifth piece, approximately 61 x 10 cm (24 x 4 in.)
- Pins
- 100 per cent cotton sewing thread
- Sewing machine
- Fabric scissors and small sharp scissors
- Iron
- Erasable fabric-marking pen
- Ruler
- Window or plastic template (see page 29)

1 Pin the first and second fabrics, right sides together as shown, and machine-stitch a straight seam. There is no need to begin or end with reverse stitching.

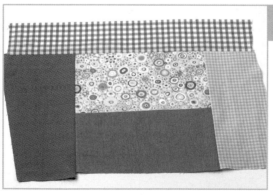

2 Trim the seam allowance to 6 mm (¼ in.) and press it to one side, as shown at right. Join the third and fourth fabrics, one at each side, in the same way. Trim and press each seam allowance as before. Join the fifth fabric along one long edge, as shown at left.

3 Use an erasable fabric-marking pen and ruler to draw a straight line anywhere across the joined pieces. Cut along the marked line.

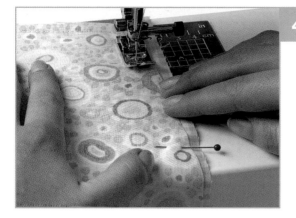

4 Turn one half around and rejoin the two halves with right sides together, as shown. If necessary, draw a straight line as a guide to stitching.

TIPS

■ The total area of fabric pieces you begin with needs to be about four times the size of the final block.

■ You can use this technique with just four fabrics, omitting the fifth fabric entirely, but it becomes more difficult to scramble them successfully. You can also use more than five fabrics, adding extra pieces at Step 2.

■ All seams must be straight; otherwise, the work will not lie flat.

■ If you want to add embroidery, tack the finished block flat onto backing fabric and work the embroidery through all of the layers.

5 Repeat Steps 3–6 several times. You can cut a straight line and rejoin the halves anywhere — try rejoining them across the middle of the piece. Trim off the excess fabric and join it elsewhere. Keep all useful-sized trimmings to one side; you can join them together to make extra strips.

6 As you continue, aim to finish with a size and shape to suit the block you want, with all of the fabrics thoroughly scrambled, as shown at left. Use a window template to mark the outline of the block, as shown below. The block is now ready for quilting or assembly.

SEE ALSO

■ Blocks and Templates, page 28
■ Machine Sewing, page 24

PINCUSHION

Every needleworker needs a pincushion, and this one is filled with sand that is contained in a separate lining to prevent leakage. Children's play sand is suitable for this project; it can be purchased from many toy stores. You can also use clean sawdust or bird sand, available from pet stores. Using smooth cotton fabrics that will not fray easily, this project can be for yourself or a gift for a friend. In this example, the confetti piecing technique has been used, but you can also use any of the piecing techniques in this book.

YOU WILL NEED

- Sewing equipment: erasable fabric-marking pen; ruler; dressmaker's shears; small, sharp scissors; straight pins; hand-sewing needle; sewing machine; iron
- Paper scissors
- 5 lightweight cotton fabric scraps, approximately 20 x 15 cm (8 x 6 in.) each
- Lightweight cotton backing fabric, 30 x 15 cm (12 x 6 in.)
- Lightweight cotton lining fabric, 30 x 15 cm (12 x 6 in.)
- Closely woven cotton inner-lining fabric, 30 x 15 cm (12 x 6 in.)
- 30 x 15 cm (12 x 6 in.) lightweight wadding
- 100 per cent cotton sewing thread to contrast with fabrics for tacking stitches
- 100 per cent cotton sewing thread to blend with fabrics for final stitching
- 100 per cent cotton sewing thread to match rayon cord
- Template plastic or cardboard
- Children's play sand, approximately 210 g (8 oz.)
- Measuring cup
- Funnel
- Thin rayon cord, 76 cm (30 in.) long
- Beads to fit around cord
- Fraycheck or fabric glue

FINISHED SIZE

- 12.5 cm (5 in.) in diameter

1 Photocopy the circular template from page 153 onto template plastic or cardboard, enlarging it by the percentage given. Cut out the template. The template's diameter should measure 14 cm (5½ in.). Using your preferred piecing technique, make a crazy-patchwork block about 30 x 15 cm (12 x 6 in.) (large enough to mark around the circle template twice). Place the 30 x 15 cm (12 x 6 in.) rectangle of lightweight cotton lining fabric right side down on a flat surface. Position the piece of lightweight wadding of the same size on top of the lining fabric, and the patchwork block on top of the wadding, right side up. Using an erasable fabric-marking pen, draw around the circle template twice onto the patchwork to give you two circles next to one another.

2 Machine-quilt as desired within the marked circles. Here, "in-the-ditch" quilting has been used along all of the seam lines, and echo quilting has been added to some of the patches.

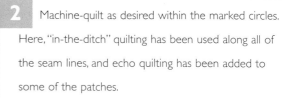

3 Use the erasable fabric-marking pen to redraw the circular outlines to make sure that they are accurate, and sew tacking stitches around each circle, just inside the marked outline. Cut out the circles following the marked outlines, as shown.

4 Position the circles right sides together and pin. Leaving a 10-cm (4-in.) opening for adding the filling later, machine-sew around the circle, leaving a seam allowance of 6 mm (¼ in.), as shown.

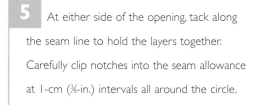

SEE ALSO
■ Confetti, page 66
■ Hand Sewing, page 20
■ Machine Sewing, page 24
■ Quilting, page 72

5 At either side of the opening, tack along the seam line to hold the layers together. Carefully clip notches into the seam allowance at 1-cm (⅜-in.) intervals all around the circle.

6 Turn the pincushion right side out.

7 Using the circle template, cut two more circles from the closely woven cotton inner-lining fabric. Following the instructions in Step 4, pin and stitch them together, leaving only a small 2.5 cm (1 in.) opening to accommodate the neck of the funnel.

8 Scoop some children's play sand into a measuring cup. Position the neck of a funnel into the opening of the inner-lining bag. Carefully pour the sand from the jug through the funnel and into the inner lining until it is about two-thirds full.

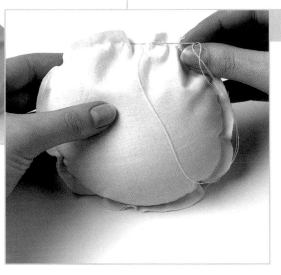

9 Pin the opening of the inner lining closed and take small, close backstitches to sew the seam line securely.

10 Slip the inner-lining pouch filled with sand inside the outer pincushion and slip-stitch by hand to close the opening, following the lines of previous tacking stitches, as shown. Remove any visible tacking stitches.

TIP

If the cord tassels are kinked, wet the strands, allow them to dry, and press with a moderate iron.

11 Take the 76-cm (30-in.) length of thin cord and form a loop at the centre. Pin the loop in position against the seam line of the pincushion. Pin the remaining cord in place all around the edge of the pincushion, as shown. Knot one end around the other, directly opposite the loop. Using cotton sewing thread to match the cord, slip-stitch the cord in place covering the seam. Stitch the loop and the knot securely in place.

12 Thread a bead onto one cord end and knot the cord to hold the bead in place. Untwist the threads of the cord up to the knot, fraying them to form a little tassel, and trim 2 cm (¾ in.) below the knot. Repeat with the other cord end. Paint the knots with Fraycheck or fabric glue and allow them time to dry.

QUILTING

Strictly speaking, quilting involves the joining together of two (or more) layers of fabric, so by that definition any kind of crazy patchwork that has a backing fabric is already "quilted." However, to obtain the three-dimensional effect associated with traditional quilting, you need to back your patchwork with a layer of wadding and an additional lining fabric.

Quilting Preparation

Whichever quilting method you choose, the preparation of the layers is the same.

1 Press the patchwork block and the lining fabric so that both lie completely flat. Lay the lining fabric on a firm, flat surface, right side down, and place the wadding on top. Place the patchwork right side up at the centre of the wadding, as shown, keeping the layers flat and smooth.

2 Beginning at the centre and working outwards, pin through all the layers out to the centre of each edge. Then pin more lines from the centre out to each corner, as shown. Turn the block over to make sure that the lining fabric remains wrinkle-free.

3 Tack along the pinned lines through all of the layers, as shown above, keeping the work flat. Work from the centre outwards. Extra grid lines may be added side to side and then up and down.

4 Your block is now prepared for quilting, by hand or machine.

"In the Ditch" Quilting by Machine

With this quilting technique, the stitches follow the seams of the patches — "in the ditch" between two patches — throwing each separate patch into low relief.

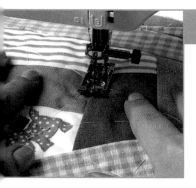

1 Set your sewing machine for straight stitch, about nine or ten stitches per 2.5 cm (1 in.). With the tension correctly adjusted, you can use one colour for the upper thread and another in the bobbin to match the lining fabric, so test stitch on a sandwich of scrap fabrics and wadding (see page 24). Beginning at the centre and working outwards, stitch along all of the patchwork seams. Do not secure the threads by reverse stitching; just leave 7.5-cm (3-in.) tails on the surface at the beginning and end of each seam. Guide your work with both hands, as shown.

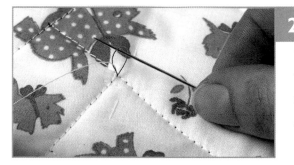

2 You can run in the thread tails as you proceed, or run them all in when you have finished stitching. Turn the block over. Pull on a bobbin-thread end, as shown, raising a little loop of top thread; catch it with a pin and pull it through.

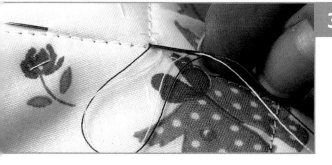

3 Thread both thread tails into a sharp embroidery needle and insert the needle where the thread emerges. Then take the needle between the layers close to the stitched line for about 2 cm (¾ in.), as shown. Bring it out again and snip off the excess threads.

4 Pull out all of the tacking stitches. Leave the block flat for a few hours to assume its natural shape. Check the size of your block outline with a window template and redraw, using an erasable fabric-marking pen, if necessary. Tack through all of the layers around the edge at the block, just inside the marked outline, and trim to the exact size required. Your quilted block is now ready for assembly into a project.

TIPS

■ For the lining fabric, choose a plain colour or a small all-over print. Avoid regular geometric patterns, such as stripes or checks, because you will not be able to line them up with the edges of your block. (You'll be stitching from the other side.)

■ Wash, dry and iron the lining fabric before you begin, to avoid shrinkage.

■ Wadding is available in several thicknesses and fibres (see page 16) to suit different uses.

■ It is important to work on a smooth, hard, flat surface. A piece of particleboard or fibreboard from a home-improvement store is a good investment because pins will scratch a polished table.

■ If your block is too large to fit easily under the sewing machine arm, roll the excess and hold it temporarily in place with clothes pegs, bicycle clips, or special clips sold for the purpose. You will need to reposition the clips for each quilting line.

Quilting by Hand

You may prefer to quilt your block by hand, especially if it is already embroidered, since tiny running stitches can be placed inconspicuously between embroidery stitches.

Mount your prepared patchwork in an embroidery hoop or frame (as on page 23), but do not stretch it too tightly. Thread a quilting needle with your chosen quilting thread and tie a knot at one end. Insert the needle through the top layer of fabric and into the wadding layer, bringing it up where required; tug gently until the knot "pops" through to the wadding layer.

METHOD 1

If your wadding is lightweight and the block is not too tightly stretched, you can pick up three or four stitches at a time, as shown at right. Hold the work so that the index finger of your non-quilting hand is underneath the stitching so you can feel the needle tip as it comes through. This method creates straighter lines and smoother curves.

METHOD 2

If your wadding is bulkier, you must make each stitch in two movements. Use a quilting needle and insert it straight down and pull it through to the back. Push the needle straight up again where required and pull it through to the top. Repeat as required. With practice this process becomes easier when you hold one hand underneath and one on top, with the hoop held in a stand.

Finish the block as shown in Step 4, page 73.

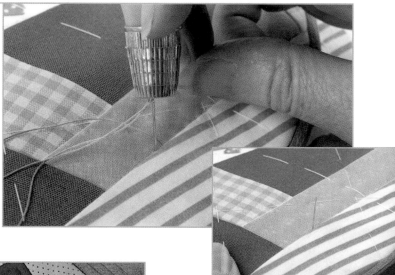

Outline and Echo Quilting

This block was quilted "in the ditch" (see page 73) and around the outline of the printed teddy bear motif. The plain patches have been "echo" quilted with lines parallel to the shape of each patch. You can draw machine-quilting guidelines for echo quilting with a ruler and erasable fabric-marking pen, or simply stitch with the outer edge of the presser foot following a seam or a previous line of stitching.

Tied Quilting

Here, the quilt layers are held together with knotted threads placed at various intervals. You can space the ties evenly in a grid formation or scatter them randomly. In either case, they should be no more than about 10 cm (4 in.) apart.

1 Thread a darning needle with an 45-cm (18-in.) length of thread, such as pearl cotton No. 5. Insert the needle where required and pull it through to the other side, leaving a tail of about 5 cm (2 in.) on the surface. Bring the needle up again about 3 mm (⅛ in.) away, and pull it through, as shown.

TIP

If your patchwork is embroidered, you can tie the knots on the reverse side of the quilted block and place them so that the stitches on the front are hidden by the embroidery.

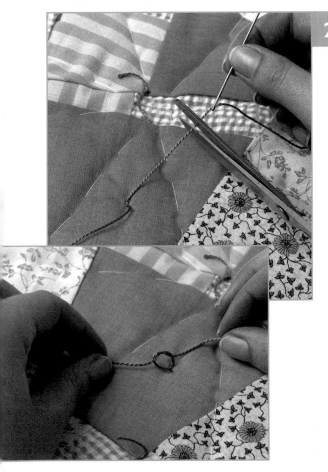

2 Hold the tail and make another small stitch, down and up again through the same holes. Pull the stitch tight and cut the working end, as shown at top left, leaving another tail of 5 cm (2 in.). Tie the two tails together using a firm reef knot (square knot), as shown at left below. Trim the tails to 1.5–2 cm (½–¾ in.). When all of the ties are in place, finish the block as shown in Step 4, page 73.

SEE ALSO
- Hand Sewing, page 20
- Machine Sewing, page 24

Button Quilting

Quilt layers may be held together by stitching on buttons arranged in a grid or randomly in the same way as ties. Flat buttons are best, since shanked buttons will sit neatly only on a very heavily padded quilt. Thread a sharp needle with a double length of sewing thread to suit the colour of the buttons. Begin with a small backstitch on the reverse side of the block and stitch firmly four or five times through each pair of holes. Fasten off with another backstitch on the wrong side and clip the thread tails close to the surface of the fabric.

CHAIR PILLOW

This cute denim pillow makes a great gift for a college student or an attractive accessory for a teenager's bedroom. Striped and checked shirt fabrics make up the crazy patchwork, using the hand-piecing technique on page 48. Simple hand embroidery embellishes the patchwork seams, and shirt buttons add the perfect finishing touch. You could make a similar cushion using any of the piecing and embroidery methods in this book, using your own choice of medium-weight fabrics.

YOU WILL NEED

- Sewing equipment: erasable fabric-marking pen; tape measure; ruler; dressmaker's shears; small, sharp scissors; straight pins; hand-sewing needle; sewing machine; iron
- 6 lightweight cotton fabric scraps, approximately 15 x 15 cm (6 x 6 in.) each
- Lightweight cotton backing fabric, 25 x 25 cm (10 x 10 in.)
- 100 per cent cotton sewing thread to contrast with fabrics for tacking stitches
- 100 per cent cotton sewing thread to blend with the fabrics for final stitching
- Embroidery thread in desired colour
- Embroidery needle to suit thread (see table, page 23)
- Shirt buttons
- Denim fabric, approximately 106 x 43 cm (42 x 17 in.)
- Blunt knitting needle or point turner
- Polyester-filled pad, 40 x 40 cm (16 x 16 in.)

FINISHED SIZE

- To fit a 40 x 40-cm (16 x 16-in.) polyester-filled pad

1 Mark a 22.5 x 22.5-cm (9 x 9-in.) square on the 25 x 25-cm (10 x 10-in.) square of lightweight cotton backing fabric. Make a patchwork block to cover the marked outline. Add hand embroidery stitches to the patchwork seams, if desired, and sew shirt buttons on the patchwork block by hand, if desired. Use the erasable fabric-marking pen to redraw the 22.5 x 22.5-cm (9 x 9-in.) square onto the right side of the patchwork. Sew tacking stitches all around, just inside the marked line; cut out the square along the marked outline, as shown.

2 From the 106 x 43-cm (42 x 17-in.) piece of denim fabric, cut two 22.5 x 11.25-cm (9 x 4 ½-in.) strips, two 42.5 x 11.25-cm (17 x 4 ½-in.) strips, and two back pieces, each measuring 43 x 30 cm (17 x 12 in.). Allowing a seam allowance of 12 mm (½ in.), pin one 22.5 x 11.25-cm (9 x 4 ½-in.) strip to one edge of the patchwork block, right sides together, and machine-sew as shown, or backstitch the seam by hand.

3 Stitch the remaining 22.5 x 11.25-cm (9 x 4 ½-in.) denim strip to the opposite edge of the patchwork block, with the same 12.5-mm (½-in.) seam allowance, and press these seam allowances open. Now pin one 43 x 11.25-cm (17 x 4 ½-in.) denim strip to each remaining side of the patchwork square. Sew the strips to the block, allowing for the same seam allowance. Press these seam allowances open.

4 The two 43 × 30-cm (17 × 12-in.) denim pieces form the overlapping pillow back. Along one long edge of each piece, fold, press and stitch a double hem, following the instructions on page 30. Lay the patchwork block, right side up on a flat surface. Place the two denim back pieces right side down on top, overlapping them to form a square to match the patchwork front. Pin through all the layers all around.

SEE ALSO

- Hand Piecing, page 48
- Hand Sewing, page 20
- Machine Sewing, page 24
- Hand Embroidery, page 22
- The Stitch Collection, page 106
- Finishing, page 30

5 Machine-sew or backstitch all around the patchwork block, using a seam allowance of 12 mm (½ in.). Clip across the corners close to the stitching line, as shown.

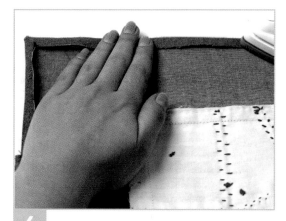

6 Press the seam allowances back all around, on both the front and the back.

7 Turn the cushion cover right side out, pushing out the corners neatly with a blunt knitting needle or a point turner. Insert a 40 × 40-cm (16 × 16-in.) polyester-filled pad to complete the project.

CRAZY LOG

This crazy version of the classic Log Cabin quilt block is fun to construct, and it is an effective way of framing a special centre patch. You can choose any fabric for the centre patch, such as the printed motif here, or a pretty piece of lace, brocade, or scrap of embroidery. The centre patch may have three, four, or five sides. This technique is suitable for either light- or medium-weight fabrics.

1 Choose your centre-patch fabric. To decide the shape of the centre patch, cut a few tapering strips from your other fabrics and arrange them around the centre patch, as shown, to make a three-, four-, or five-sided shape. When you are pleased with your results, mark the inside corners with dots using an erasable fabric-marking pen.

YOU WILL NEED

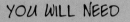

- Fabrics (light- or medium-weight), including one to act as the centre patch
- Erasable fabric-marking pen
- Ruler
- Fabric scissors and small, sharp scissors
- Window or plastic template (see page 29)
- Backing fabric, at least 2.5 cm (1 in.) larger all around than required block
- Straight pins
- 100 per cent cotton sewing thread
- Sewing machine
- Iron
- Small sewing needle

2 Use a ruler and an erasable fabric-marking pen to join the dots and cut out the centre patch 6 mm (¼ in.) outside these lines, as shown.

3 Use the fabric-marking pen and a window template to mark the outline of the block on the backing fabric. Arrange the centre patch, right side up, at the centre and pin it in place. Place the first strip, right side down, on top of the centre patch, matching one edge, as shown. Pin and machine-stitch 6 mm (¼ in.) from the raw edges. Stitch only where there are three fabric layers – backing, centre patch and first strip. There is no need to secure the thread ends.

4 If necessary, trim the edge of the centre patch to match the first strip so it cannot show through as a dark "shadow." Flip the strip over, right side up, and press. Working clockwise or anticlockwise, as desired, position the next strip, as shown. The second strip should be long enough to cover the next side of the centre patch and the short end of the first strip.

TIPS

■ All seams must be perfectly straight; otherwise, the work will not lie flat. Sometimes it helps to draw a straight guideline for stitching using a ruler and an erasable fabric-marking pen.

■ If you prefer to stitch by hand, you can backstitch the seams instead of machine stitching them.

5 Stitch the second seam, as before, and trim the edges to match the new strip. (You may need to unpick a few stitches of the previous seam.) Flip the new strip over, right side up, and press. Add more strips in the same way. Each new strip must be long enough to cover one long edge and the short ends of any adjacent strips; you can join two pieces to make a longer strip, if necessary. The tapering strips can be arranged wide end first, narrow end first, or a mixture of the two.

6 Continue adding more strips until the block outline is completely covered, with no gaps. Use the window template to mark the outline of the block and tack all around the outside edges, just inside the marked line. The block is now ready for quilting, embroidery, or assembly.

SEE ALSO:
■ Blocks and Templates, page 28
■ Machine Sewing, page 24
■ Hand Sewing, page 20

Three-Sided Variation
The central piece of lace here has been backed with contrasting silk and the strips added in a three-sided arrangement.

Five-Sided Variation
This fragment of antique embroidery suits a five-sided shape, with strips in soft shades of blue.

RIBBONS AND TRIMS

Ribbons, lace, broderie anglaise and other fabric trims can be set into the seams of crazy patchwork as the patches are stitched in place. They may be cut to match the length of the seam and added flat, or cut longer and gathered into a ruffle. They may also be added after the piecing is finished in the form of rosettes, flowers and other three-dimensional decorations.

To Make a Ruffle

YOU WILL NEED

Along with the usual patchwork equipment, depending on the patchwork method you have chosen, you will also need:

- Trims, in the form of ribbons, lace, or broderie anglaise
- Seam ripper, if using the trim-seams-after-patching technique
- 100 per cent cotton sewing thread
- Small hand sewing needle

1 A plain ribbon or fine lace often looks more decorative if it is gathered into a ruffle. Cut a piece of trim one and a half times as long as the edge of the patch to be trimmed. Thread a small, sharp needle with sewing thread and knot one end of the thread. Begin at one end of the trim, close to one long edge (the raw edge, if there is one), and take the needle up and down in a straight line, making running stitches about 3 mm (⅛ in.) long all along the edge, as shown.

2 Pull gently on the thread to gather the trim to match the length you require. Secure the thread with two small backstitches. Arrange the fullness evenly. The ruffle may be added to a patch by following the trim-seams-as-you-patch method, or the trim-seams-after-patching method, both shown opposite.

Trim-Seams-As-You-Patch Method

This technique is suitable for sew-and-flip, strip-piecing and crazy-log techniques (see pages 40, 54 and 78). When hand piecing (see page 48), follow Step 1, tack the trim in place, then add the next patch as usual. Trims may be added flat, as shown, or gathered, as opposite.

1 Pin one long edge of the trim, right side up, to the edge of the previous patch. If the trim is gathered, the gathered edge should lie along the edge of the patch. Insert pins at right angles to the edge to hold the trim in place, as shown.

2 Pin the new patch, right side down, and stitch the seam through all of the layers. For a ruffle, there is no need to remove the running stitches if they are hidden inside the seam allowance. When you flip the new patch over to press it, the trim will be secured by the seam and lie on top of the lower patch. As you add more patches, the raw ends of the trim will be hidden.

Trim-Seams-After-Patching Method

Sometimes it's easier to add trims at a later stage so you can choose them to suit the patches. If you are hand piecing (see page 48), you can piece and tack the whole block; then unpick the tacking to add trims where desired. You can unpick machine-stitched, backstitched, or slip-stitched seams in a similar way to add a trim to any type of crazy patchwork (except fusible-web, see page 60), although unpicking machine stitching can be a time-consuming task.

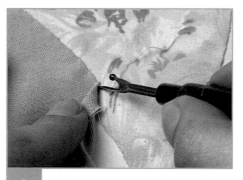

1 Use a seam ripper to carefully unpick a seam or tacking. You may need to make gaps in adjacent seams, too, to hide the raw ends of your trim.

2 If desired, gather the trim, as shown on the opposite page; then, tuck the gathered edge into the open seam and tuck the ends under adjacent patches, as shown above.

3 Pin and tack the patch back into place, ready for hand stitching or embroidery.

To Ruche a Trim

To ruche a ribbon, first gather it with running stitches in a similar way to Step 1 of "To Make a Ruffle," as shown on page 80, but following a zigzag path. Gently pull on the thread to ruche the ribbon to the required length and fasten off the thread with two backstitches. Ruched ribbons may be sewn to the patchwork with tiny stitches hidden in the folds or held down with embroidery stitches.

To Fold a Bow

Fold a 10-cm (4-in.) length of 1-cm (⅜-in.)-wide ribbon and use matching thread to hold the folds in place with two or three small stitches. Sew where desired on your patchwork, adding a bead or sequin to hide the stitches.

To Make a Single Rosette

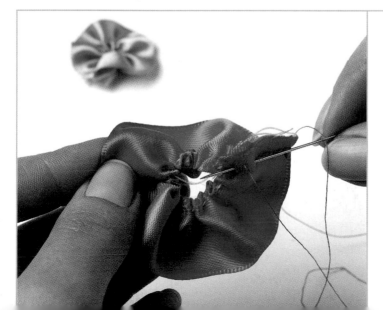

Work a line of running stitches along a length of ribbon or lace following Step 1 of "To Make a Ruffle" (see page 80); then join the two ends with a small seam, making a ring, as shown at left. Gather up tightly and secure the gathering thread; use this thread to sew the rosette where desired on your patchwork. You can also add beads or embroidery stitches at the centre, if desired.

To Make a Double Rosette

Follow the technique for a single rosette (opposite), but run the gathering thread along the centre of the ribbon instead of along one edge.

SEE ALSO

- Hand Sewing, page 20
- Machine Sewing, page 24
- Beads, Sequins, and Mirrors, page 84
- Hand Embroidery, page 22
- Machine Embroidery, page 26

Purchased Decorations

Machine-embroidered appliqué motifs may be purchased in a wide range of designs. Pin the motif where required and backstitch all around with tiny stitches, using thread to match the motif. Ric-rac and other braids may be machine-stitched along the centre with matching or contrasting thread.

BEADS, SEQUINS AND MIRRORS

All kinds of embellishments may be added to your patchwork. As a rule, it is easier to add bulky decorations, such as large beads, at the end of a project, but for a small, complicated project, such as a purse with a lining, it is often easier to add them before completing the assembly.

You can sew decorations in place with small, almost invisible stitches or attach them with contrasting embroidery stitches (see page 132).

Sewing on Beads

Beads are available in a wide range of sizes. You can use small beads to add texture to a patch, add them to flower centres, or stitch them in straight or curved lines to make patterns.

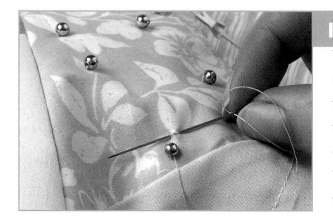

I Choose a small, sharp needle that fits easily through your bead. Thread it with 100 per cent cotton sewing thread in a colour to match the bead. Double thread is advisable for larger beads. Bring the needle up through the fabric where required, leaving a short thread tail (just long enough to hold in place with your finger) on the wrong side, and make a tiny backstitch on the surface. Thread the bead onto the needle and make another small stitch through the fabric in the same place, as shown.

YOU WILL NEED

Along with the usual patchwork equipment, depending on the patchwork method you have chosen, you will also need:

■ Beads, sequins, shisha mirrors, or any decorative charms

■ Small sewing needle to fit through bead or sequin

■ 100 per cent cotton sewing thread

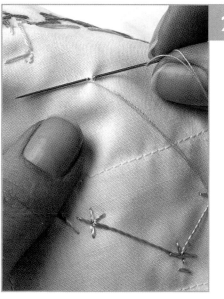

2 Tighten the stitch gently so that the bead sits neatly on the fabric. Pass the needle through the bead again and through the fabric to the wrong side. Make another tiny backstitch on the wrong side, behind the bead, as shown. If you are sewing on several beads, you can move on to another bead position close by without cutting the thread, beginning with another backstitch in the new position.

Sewing on Sequins with Beads

Sequins are metallic foil shapes with small holes punched for sewing onto fabric. They are often circular, but stars, flowers and other shapes are also available. If they are sewn on with small stitches in a similar way to beads, the stitches will be visible, even in closely matching thread. Another method is to sew them on with beads so that the stitches cannot be seen.

TIPS

■ Along with beads, sequins and shisha mirrors, all kinds of charms pierced with holes for stitching are available to suit different themes and occasions. Pretty buttons can also be used, but avoid those with shanks, since they will not sit flat on the fabric surface (unless it is heavily quilted). Buttons with holes are usually more suitable.

■ As a rule, choose thread to match the bead, sequin, charm or button rather than to match the fabric.

1 Choose a thread to match the bead. Secure the thread in the same way as in "Sewing on Beads" (opposite) and bring the needle through to the right side of the work where required. Make a tiny backstitch on the surface, thread on a sequin, then thread on a tiny bead, as shown.

2 Take the needle back to the wrong side through the hole in the sequin, as shown. The sequin is secured by the bead, and the thread is hardly visible. Repeat the process of stitching through the bead and sequin for extra strength before securing the thread with another backstitch on the wrong side.

Sewing on Shisha Mirrors

These cute little mirrors with gilt borders are called "shisha." They come in two pieces: a mirrored disk and a stitchable, woven wire ring to hold each mirror in place. Originally from India, they add bold sparkle to any embroidery.

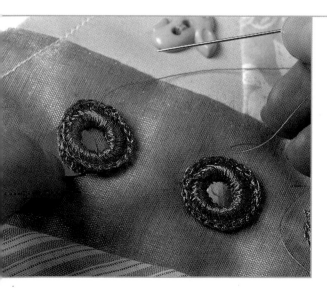

Choose a 100 per cent cotton sewing thread to match the border ring, such as yellow for gold rings and palest grey for silver. Thread a small, sharp needle and secure the thread with a small backstitch on the wrong side of the work. Hold the outer ring in place on the surface and bring the needle through just inside the outer edge. Stitch one third of the outer edge in place with tiny backstitches; then slip the mirror into place, as shown. Complete the stitching all around and secure the thread with backstiches on the wrong side of the fabric.

SEE ALSO

■ Hand Sewing, page 20
■ Stitches for Sequins and Beads, page 132

PHOTOGRAPH ALBUM COVER

A wonderful way to celebrate the arrival of a new baby is to make a crazy-patchwork cover for a photograph album. You could also adapt this design for a wedding, vacation, or anniversary album. The patchwork block shown here was made using the crazy-log technique on page 78, incorporating a photograph printed onto fabric and a selection of lightweight cotton and silk fabrics: Lace, ribbons, beads and other trims add elegance. Enjoy using any of the piecing techniques featured in this book to make your own personal album cover.

1 Measure the height of your photograph album. Make a note of this measurement *plus* 3 cm (1¼ in.).

2 With the album closed, measure from the front edge all the way around to the back edge. This measurement *plus* 3 cm (1¼ in.), plus the measurement noted in Step 1, gives you the size of patchwork block you need to make, including a seam allowance of 12 mm (½ in.) all around, plus 3 mm (⅛ in.) all around to allow for the width of the end boards.

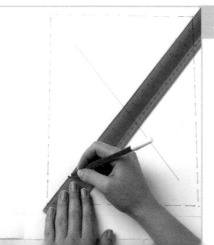

3 Using the measurements gathered in Steps 1–2, mark the correct size patchwork block outline on a piece of cotton backing fabric that is at least 5 cm (2 in.) larger all around than your album measurements. Mark a dashed outline of the actual size of the front of the album cover at one end, then find the centre of this front area by drawing two diagonal lines from corner to corner, as shown.

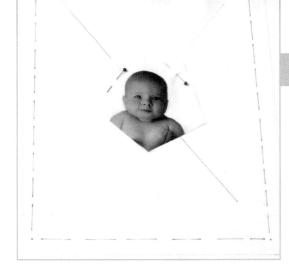

4 Following the manufacturer's instructions, use the photo-transfer medium to transfer a photograph of your choice onto a piece of white cotton fabric. Use this as the starting point of the crazy patchwork, positioning the photograph patch at the centre point of the front piece marked on your backing fabric, as shown.

5 Complete the entire patchwork block for the album, using your preferred piecing technique. Add some hand embroidery and decorative embellishments as desired. Use the erasable fabric-marking pen to redraw the outline of the block size from Step 2 onto the right side of the patchwork block. Sew tacking stitches all around the block, just inside the marked outline, and cut out the block, following the outline, as shown.

6 Cut the 51-cm (20-in.)-length of 2.5-cm (1-in.)-wide ribbon in half and pin one half at the centre of each short side edge of the patchwork block, as shown.

7 Cut three pieces of lining fabric, each the same height as the finished patchwork block and a width that is one-third of that of the finished patchwork block *plus* 5 cm (2 in.). To make the centre section, turn and stitch a single hem, 12 mm (½ in.) wide along both long sides of one of the pieces of lining fabric. Turn and stitch a similar hem along one long side of each of the remaining sections.

SEE ALSO
- Crazy Log, page 78
- Hand Sewing, page 20
- Machine Sewing, page 24
- Hand Embroidery, page 22
- The Stitch Collection, page 106
- Ribbons and Trims, page 80
- Beads, Sequins and Mirrors, page 84

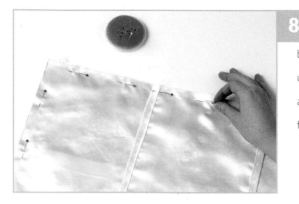

8 Arrange the lining pieces on top of the patchwork block with right sides together and the centre section uppermost. Overlap the hemmed edges. Pin all around as shown and sew tacking stitches 12 mm (½ in.) in from the edges.

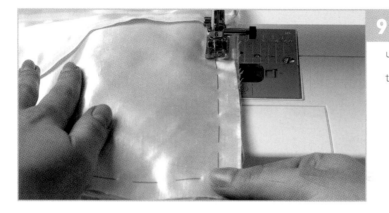

9 Machine-sew or backstitch by hand all around, using a 12 mm (½ in.) seam allowance. Remove the tacking stitches.

10 Clip across the corners, close to the stitching line. Take care not to cut through the seam stitches.

11 Fold the seam allowances back on both sides, all around, and press.

12 Turn the album cover right side out, pushing out the corners neatly with the blunt knitting needle or point turner, and press carefully.

14 Trim the ribbon ends on the diagonal to prevent fraying. You may also want to paint them with a little Fraycheck or fabric glue.

13 Slip the cover onto the album.

TIPS

■ When transferring your photograph to fabric, the process will depend on the product you use, so follow the manufacturer's instructions carefully. You can cut away any unwanted parts of the image before transferring it; it's a good idea to use these as test pieces before transferring the actual photograph.

■ Take care never to touch the transferred photograph with a hot iron, because it might melt.

■ Never pin through the transferred photograph surface, because this will leave permanent holes in the fabric.

■ If your finished album cover is rather loose, cut a piece of lightweight wadding to size and insert it, flat, between the album and the cover on both front and back.

PAPER-TEMPLATE PIECING

Use this technique if you want to design your block carefully before you start. You can make several blocks with the same arrangement of patches, choosing identical fabrics for each block, or varying the fabrics within the same patch arrangement. You can piece the patches using either the sew-and-flip (see page 40), hand-piecing (see page 48), strip-piecing technique (see page 54), or fusible web (see page 60).

YOU WILL NEED

- Paper and pencil
- Fine black pen
- Ruler
- Eraser
- Lightweight cardboard
- Paper and fabric scissors
- Fabrics for patchwork
- Erasable fabric-marking pen
- Quilter's quarter (optional)
- Backing fabric, at least 2.5 cm (1 in.) larger all around than block
- Patchwork equipment, as required for piecing method you have chosen

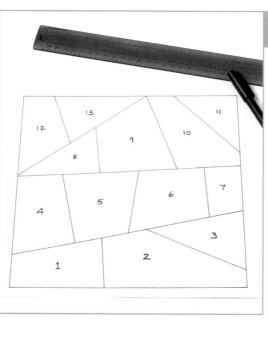

I Use a pencil to draw or trace the outline of the block accurately onto the paper. Sketching lightly, divide the block into patches, as desired. When you are happy with the arrangement, draw over all the patch lines and the block outline with a fine, black marking pen and ruler and erase the pencil marks. Number each patch, as shown. Make a photocopy of your design onto lightweight cardboard and keep the original to use as a reference for positioning the numbered patches.

2 Cut the photocopy into individual patches. Place each cardboard shape, numbered side down, on the wrong side of the appropriate fabric and draw around each one with an erasable pen. Cut the fabric 6 mm (¼ in.) larger all around than the marked shape. For extra accuracy you can use a quilter's quarter, as shown at left, to mark these 6 mm (¼ in.) seam allowances on each shape. Number the patches as you mark them with the erasable fabric-marking pen.

3 Use the erasable fabric-marking pen to trace the block design onto the backing fabric. Be sure to mark the outline and the lines of each patch, numbering them, as in Step 1. Elongate the lines around each shape, so that you can line up the seams of the patch correctly.

TIPS

■ Photocopy sections of large designs onto separate sheets of cardboard and tape them together to form the whole design.

■ You can also make photocopies on a computer with a scanner.

■ If you do not have access to a photocopier or a scanner, make an accurate tracing of your design to keep as a reference.

■ Cutting paper soon blunts scissors, so keep a separate pair for this purpose.

4 Position each patch on the marked backing fabric, as shown. Each patch should overlap the corresponding shape on the backing fabric by 6 mm (¼ in.) all around, with the seam lines (not the outside edges) matching the design lines of the block, as shown. Complete the patchwork by your chosen method.

You can use the cardboard shapes to make more blocks. These can be identical, with the same fabrics and embroidery, or you can vary the colours and decoration while keeping the patch arrangement exactly the same.

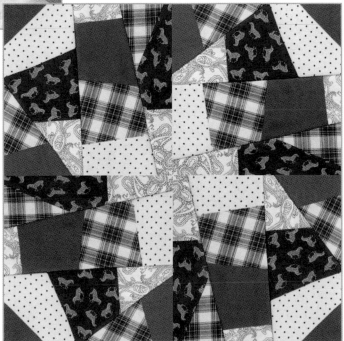

SEE ALSO

■ Sew-and-Flip, page 40
■ Hand Piecing, page 48
■ Strip Piecing, page 54
■ Fusible Web, page 60

ASSEMBLING A QUILT

Assembling a quilt top in the best way possible starts at the planning stage and continues through the piecing of blocks and/or strips right up to the layering of the quilt sandwich. To make sure all of your quilts are straight, with accurate corners, follow these simple steps.

Parts of a Quilt

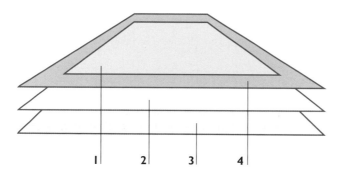

1 QUILT TOP The top layer of a quilt sandwich, usually assembled from several blocks and/or strips.

2 WADDING The middle layer of wadding gives the quilt warmth and loft.

3 LINING A thin layer of fabric is required beneath the wadding. A lightweight cotton fabric, plain or printed, suits most quilts.

4 BORDERS There are several ways to border a quilt. Use a lightweight plain cotton fabric in a fairly strong colour that matches or blends with the patchwork.

1 Plan the size of your quilt carefully before you begin to piece the top. For a bed quilt, measure the mattress top and add a suitable overhang – at least 20 cm (8 in.) – to both sides and the bottom edge. A quilted throw or wall hanging can be any size you wish. Large quilt tops are usually made in blocks, which are joined together after patching. The border of a quilt can be any width, from 12 mm (½ in.) to 10 or 15 cm (4 or 6 in.) or more, depending on the size of the quilt centre. Sketch a few arrangements to scale on graph paper, as shown, and decide on a suitable block size and border width to give your quilt the measurements you desire.

2 Remember to include a seam allowance in each block. A seam allowance of 12 mm (½ in) is shown on these pages. Piece the blocks by whatever patchwork method you wish. Then redraw the block outline accurately, as shown, and tack all around the outside edge, just inside the marked outline. Work any hand embroidery at this stage. Cut out the block. Repeat for all blocks in your quilt.

3 Lay the blocks out on a flat surface and try arranging them in different ways. When you are happy with the arrangement, lightly number the blocks with the erasable fabric-marking pen, as shown, working from left to right and top to bottom.

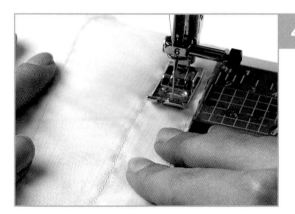

4 Join the blocks into strips; then join the strips together to form the quilt top. To join two blocks, lay them flat, with right sides together, matching all the raw edges exactly. Pin along the seam to be joined. (For slippery fabrics, tacking may be advisable.) Stitch the seam with an accurate seam allowance.

5 Press along the seam to set the stitches; then press the seam allowance open. Join all of the blocks into strips and pin two strips, right sides together, matching the previous seams exactly, as shown. Tack if necessary, and stitch the seam. Press the seam allowance open, as before.

6 Join all of the strips in the same way to complete the quilt top. Your quilt top is now ready for quilting.

YOU WILL NEED

- Tape measure
- Graph paper and pen or pencil
- Patchwork equipment, depending on the patchwork method you have chosen
- Erasable fabric-marking pen
- 100 per cent cotton sewing thread
- Sewing machine
- Iron
- Backing fabric
- Wadding
- Quilting equipment (see page 72)
- Fabric for binding
- Long ruler or yardstick

TIPS

- Pieces of backing fabric may be joined to make up any backing size required. Trim off any selvages and join the pieces with right sides together, with straight seams. Press these seams open.

- Pieces of wadding may also be joined to make a larger size bolt. Lay the wadding pieces flat, with the edges butted together (not overlapping) and stitch them together by hand with large zigzag stitches to make a flat join. When the wadding is quilted, these joins will be secure.

7 Cut the wadding and backing fabric about 5 cm (2 in.) larger all around than the size of the finished quilt top, including borders. Place the backing wrong side up on a flat surface, and centre the wadding on top. Position the quilt top at the centre, as shown. Tack the layers together and quilt by hand or machine, as desired (see page 72). Tack all around the quilt sandwich, just inside the raw edges and cut away the excess wadding and backing fabric.

8 For the double binding, cut strips of fabric on the cross or lengthways grain of the fabric. The width of these strips should be six times the width of the desired finished binding width, so for a 5-cm (2-in.)-wide binding you will need strips that are 30 cm (12 in.) wide. Cut two strips to match the two sides of your quilt top and cut two more strips to the length of the top and bottom edges *plus* 2.5 cm (1 in.). Fold each strip in half lengthways, with wrong sides together, and press the fold firmly, as shown.

SEE ALSO
- Quilting, page 72
- Machine Sewing, page 24
- Hand Sewing, page 20

9 On each doubled strip use a long ruler and erasable fabric-marking pen to mark a stitching line, one binding width in from the raw edges, as shown. Take one strip (length to match side of quilt) and pin it to one side of the quilt, matching the raw edges. Stitch through all thicknesses along the marked line.

10 Press the binding away from the quilt top and fold it over to the back. Depending on the thickness of your wadding, you may need to trim the quilt edge slightly: The folded edge of the binding should meet the line of stitching on the back of the quilt. Pin it in place, as shown, and slip-stitch (see page 21) the folded edge to the back of the previous stitching line. Bind the opposite edge of the quilt top in the same way.

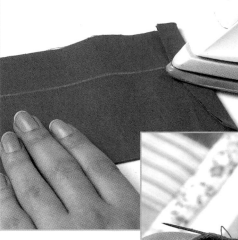

11 Bind the top and bottom edges of the quilt sandwich with the two longer strips. Take one of these strips and press 12 mm (½ in.) in at each end, as shown at left, above. Apply the binding strip to the top edge as Step 9, with the folded ends uppermost. Fold it over and slip-stitch the binding to the back as in Step 10. Slip-stitch the folded edges together at the corners, as shown at left, below. Bind the remaining edge in the same way.

TIPS

■ "Double binding" is made from separate straight strips of fabric (see Steps 8–11, pages 94–95).

■ "Self-binding" is made by cutting the backing fabric larger all around and folding it over to the front of the quilt (see Baby Quilt, page 96).

■ You can purchase commercial bias binding in a wide range of colours and several widths. Apply this as shown on page 31.

Adding a Hanging Sleeve

One way to hang a quilt on a wall is to add a tubular hanging sleeve to the back. Then you can slip a dowel or pole through the sleeve and rest the ends of the pole on nails or hooks. The quilt will hang straight, without sagging. Plan your hangings with generous borders to hide the sleeve and pole.

1 Bind the side edges first, following Steps 8–10, opposite. Cut a straight strip of backing fabric, of a length to match the top quilt edge and a width to fit easily around the pole, plus 2.5 cm (1 in.) for seam allowances. A strip that is 11.5 cm (4½ in.) wide will fit a pole diameter of 2.5 cm (1 in.). Fold and press the short ends of the strip to the wrong side by 12 mm (½ in.) and stitch them down with zigzag stitch. Fold the strip in half with wrong sides together and pin it to the wrong side of the quilt, at the centre of the top edge, so that the raw edges are 12 mm (½ in.) above the line where you will machine stitch the binding in place.

2 Tack the hanging sleeve in place, stitching about 1 cm (⅜ in.) from the raw edges. Then apply the binding to the top and bottom edges of the quilt, as Step 11, above.

BABY QUILT

This lovely little quilt has the appearance of being a single large block. However, the quilt top is actually made in four blocks using the sew-and-flip method (see page 40), with some patches overlapping the seams to disguise them. The borders are made by cutting the quilt lining larger than the quilt top and folding the lining over to the front to form the borders. This method of bordering, called "self-binding," is suitable only for a quilt size that will fit within the lining-fabric width. A baby quilt should be easy to launder, so choose solid-coloured or cotton fabrics and cotton wadding, and be sure to wash all of the fabrics separately before you begin.

I Using the erasable fabric-marking pen, mark 43 x 68.5-cm (17 x 27-in.) outlines for the four crazy-patchwork blocks onto the pieces of backing fabric. The marked size includes a seam allowance of 12 mm (½ in.) all around. Arrange and piece the four patchwork blocks using the sew-and-flip method on page 40, but on two adjacent sides of each block, leave one or two overhanging patches untrimmed. It is actually a good idea to leave all four blocks incomplete along two adjacent edges so that they can be arranged together, as shown, before planning which patches will overlap the seams between blocks.

2 Add machine-embroidered flowers and stars, using the designs on page 134.

3 On a flat surface, line up the four patchwork blocks to form roughly the final quilt shape. Press the free edges of the overlapping patch(es) to the wrong side by 6 mm (¼ in.), as shown. Machine- or hand-sew the fixed edge in place. Leave any parts inside the block seam allowance areas unstitched. Pin the overlapping patch(es) back.

4 Check the measurements of the four patchwork blocks (in case they have been distorted by the stitching and embroidery); then join them together, following the instructions on page 93, Steps 4–6. Flip the overlapping patch(es) over, as shown.

5 Draw around each overlapping patch on the right side of the patchwork block using the erasable fabric-marking pen. Trim away the excess fabric below it, 6 mm (¼ in.) inside the marked outline, as shown.

SEE ALSO
- Sew-and-Flip, page 40
- Hand Sewing, page 20
- Machine Sewing, page 24
- Machine Embroidery, page 26
- Machine-embroidery Stitches, page 134
- Quilting, page 72

6 Pin and tack the overlapping patches in place and slip-stitch by hand, as shown, using thread to match the patches. Add more embroidery, if desired.

7 The quilt top should now measure 84 × 134.5 cm (33 × 53 in.). Prepare the quilt top, medium-weight cotton wadding, and lightweight cotton lining fabric for quilting, following the instructions on page 72, positioning the wadding at the centre of the lining fabric, and the quilt top at the centre of the wadding. Using the erasable fabric-marking pen, draw a seam line all around the outside edge, 12 mm (½ in.) in from the edge on all sides of the quilt top, as shown.

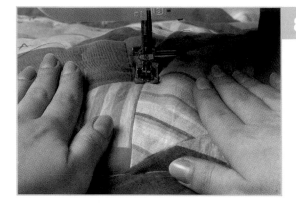

8 Machine-quilt through all of the layers, as shown, following the instructions on page 73. Here, a wide zigzag stitch and an automatic embroidery stitch resembling blanket stitch are being used. End all of your quilting lines 3 mm (⅛ in.) outside the marked outline.

9 You don't have to quilt along all of the patchwork seams, as shown, but however you quilt, the lines of stitching should be spaced no more than 15 cm (6 in.) apart. Remove all of the tacking stitches except those around the outside edge. Run all of the thread ends into the wadding layer.

10 Measure and mark a line on the wadding 7.5 cm (3 in.) outside the seam line, marked in Step 7, on all sides of the quilt. Trim the wadding only to this size, as shown. Check to make sure that the lining fabric is 9 cm (3½ in.) larger than the wadding all around the quilt.

11 Fold the raw edge of the lining fabric in by 12 mm (½ in.) along the two short edges of the quilt, then fold it again to meet the marked seam line. Pin and tack in place, as shown.

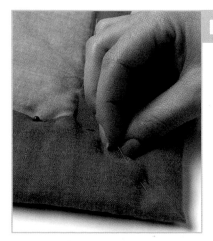

12 Fold in the long edges as in Step 11, with the corners folded under to make mitres, as shown. Pin and tack these edges and corners.

13 Stitching through the quilt top only, without stitching through to the lining, slip-stitch all around the border and corner seams by hand, as shown, using thread to match the lining fabric.

14 Quilt all around the edge of the border using a wide zigzag stitch, as shown, with the inner edge of the zigzag line falling "in the ditch" between the border and the quilt top. Remove all visible tacking stitches and mist traces of erasable fabric-marking pen with water. If necessary, steam the quilt gently with no pressure on the iron, then leave the quilt flat for a few hours to dry.

TIP

Although it is easier to add embroidery before the patchwork blocks are assembled, you can add more embroidery at any stage if you need to balance the arrangement. Once the quilt layers are assembled, machine embroidery must be worked through all of the layers, while hand embroidery may be carefully added without stitching through to the lining.

SIGN AND DATE YOUR QUILT

Sign and date your quilt for the benefit of future owners. This is usually done on a label attached to the back of the quilt, but this information can be added anywhere you choose. There are two ways to do this. You can make a machine- or hand-stitched label, turn the edges under, and stitch it in place on the quilt back, or embroider by hand directly onto the lining fabric or on top of one of the patches. Include the date and your name or initials. For a baby quilt it's a nice idea to include baby's name and date of birth.

WORKING WITH PAPER PATTERNS

Crazy patchwork is suitable for making toys, hats, purses and other accessories – even a simple jacket – providing you choose a suitable pattern. Most projects (except stuffed toys) will need to be lined to hide and protect the seams.

SPECIAL NOTES

■ Patterns for stretch fabrics are not suitable.

■ The lightest-weight patchwork you could make would use fine silks on a silk organza backing, forming an equivalent to light- to medium-weight fabric. Whatever patching technique you use, the resulting patchwork will be heavier than the fabrics you start with, so choose your pattern and fabrics accordingly.

■ Choose a simple pattern with a minimum of pattern pieces and seams. Avoid designs with sewn details, such as darts and gathers. Consider cutting some pieces from plain fabric; for example, you could make a waistcoat with crazy patchwork fronts and a plain fabric back.

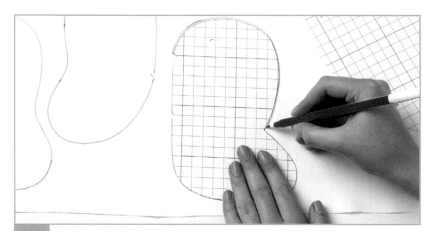

1 Cut out the paper pattern pieces along the solid outlines and lay them out on the backing fabric, allowing space for duplicates if necessary. Pattern pieces are normally marked with arrows that match the straight grain (or nap) of the fabric; you can ignore these, because your finished patchwork will be stable. Position the pieces about 2.5 cm (1 in.) apart in any order you choose. Pin large pattern pieces in place. Use an erasable marking pen to draw around each one, as shown above. Mark the position of such details as notches, buttonholes, toy eyes or seam openings.

YOU WILL NEED

■ Paper pattern
■ Paper and fabric scissors
■ Backing fabric
■ Pins
■ Erasable fabric marker
■ Fabrics for patchwork
■ Patchwork equipment required for the piecing method you have chosen

2 If you wish, cut between the outlines of the marked shapes to work on each piece separately, leaving a margin of at least 12 mm (½ in.) around each. Now work the patchwork by your chosen method to cover the entire shape. There should be at least 6 mm (¼ in.) of the patchwork overlapping the marked lines. Try to avoid placing bulky seams at marked points such as buttonholes and eye positions. Avoid joining more than two fabrics anywhere within the seam allowance. (Your pattern pieces will tell you how wide this allowance is on each piece.) Press the patchwork carefully.

3 Replace each pattern piece on the right side of the patchwork, face down, and mark around it. You can adjust the positions of the pieces slightly at this stage, if necessary, to make the arrangement of patches more pleasing or to avoid placing a patchwork seam in an awkward place.

4 Tack all around the outline of each piece just inside the marked outline, as shown.

5 Work any embroidery or quilting required. Hand-embroidery threads should be secured within the outline of each shape to avoid cutting through them later.

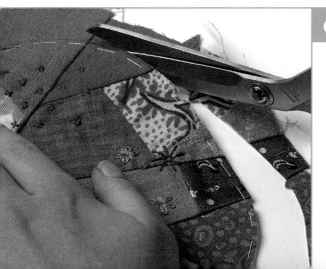

6 Cut each of the pattern pieces out along the marked lines. Now you are ready to assemble the project, following the instructions supplied with your pattern. Remove the tacking after stitching the assembly seams.

TIPS

■ Small pattern pieces may be photocopied onto thin cardboard and cut out to make templates that are much easier to handle than paper.

■ Where a pattern piece indicates that it should be placed on a fold of fabric, use a ruler to draw a straight line to represent the fold, draw around the piece, then flip it over to draw the second half.

■ If you want to use the confetti technique on page 66, make one or more large blocks sufficient to cut out the pattern pieces. When placing the paper pattern pieces, try to avoid placing seam allowances (and details such as buttonholes) over the corners of patches, where the seams can be bulky.

SEE ALSO
■ Hand Sewing, page 20
■ Machine Embroidery, page 26
■ Hand Embroidery, page 22
■ Quilting, page 72

TEDDY BEAR

You can make this cuddly patchwork bear in bright cottons or more decorative fabrics, such as velveteen or corduroy. The sew-and-flip technique has been used for this project, but you might prefer to try hand piecing (see page 48).

YOU WILL NEED

- Paper scissors
- Thin cardboard or graph paper
- Lightweight cotton backing fabric, 50 x 76 cm (20 x 30 in.)
- Sewing equipment: erasable fabric-marking pen; tape measure; ruler; dressmaker's shears; small, sharp scissors; straight pins; hand-sewing needle; sewing machine; iron
- 10 lightweight cotton fabric scraps, approximately 30 x 30 cm (12 x 12 in.) each
- 100 per cent cotton sewing thread to contrast with fabrics for tacking stitches
- 100 per cent cotton sewing thread to blend with fabrics for final stitching
- Embroidery thread in desired colours
- Embroidery needle to suit the thread used (see table, page 23)
- Polyester fibrefill
- Large darning needle or 12.5 cm (5 in.) doll needle
- Two black buttons
- 100 per cent black cotton sewing thread to blend with buttons
- Black pearl cotton, No. 5
- Ribbon, 50 cm (20 in.) long and 2.5 cm (1 in.) wide

FINISHED SIZE

- Height 40.5 cm (16 in.)

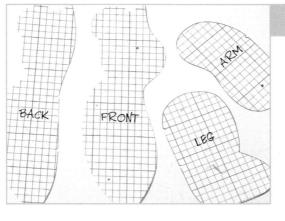

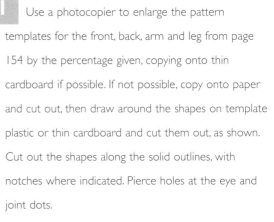

1 Use a photocopier to enlarge the pattern templates for the front, back, arm and leg from page 154 by the percentage given, copying onto thin cardboard if possible. If not possible, copy onto paper and cut out, then draw around the shapes on template plastic or thin cardboard and cut them out, as shown. Cut out the shapes along the solid outlines, with notches where indicated. Pierce holes at the eye and joint dots.

2 Using the erasable fabric-marking pen, draw around the front template onto lightweight cotton backing fabric. Turn the template over and position it 2.5 cm (1 in.) away from the first shape. Draw around the reversed template. Repeat this process to draw two backs (one in reverse), four arms (two in reverse), and four legs (two in reverse). Mark the eye and joint dots through the pierced holes.

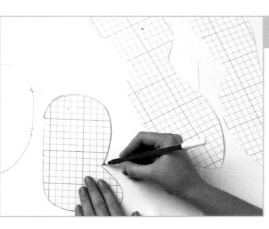

3 Use your preferred piecing technique to make crazy-patchwork blocks to cover each of the backing-fabric shapes, as shown, overlapping the marked outlines by *at least* 6 mm (¼ in.) all around. It is a good idea to avoid placing patchwork seams over the eye dots.

4 Using the erasable fabric-marking pen, redraw the outline of each shape onto the appropriate patchwork units, and remark the eye and joint dots. Add some simple hand embroidery, securing the threads within the outline of each piece.

5 Tack all around each piece, 3 mm (⅛ in.) inside the marked outline. Cut out all of the pieces along the marked lines, as shown. Decide which arm and leg pieces to pair together.

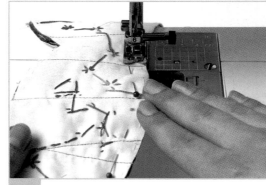

6 Place the two front patchwork pieces right sides together and pin the centre-front seam from the point at the top of the head to the base. Machine-sew the seam, as shown, or backstitch it by hand, with a 1 cm (⅜ in.) seam allowance.

SEE ALSO

- Sew-and-Flip, page 40
- Hand Sewing, page 20
- Machine Sewing, page 24
- Hand Embroidery, page 22
- The Stitch Collection, page 106

7 Place the two back patchwork pieces right sides together and pin the centre back seam. Machine-sew or backstitch the seam with a 1-cm (⅜-in.) seam allowance, leaving a 8 cm (3¼ in.) opening between the two notches, as shown.

8 Place the front and back pieces right sides together, matching the centre front and back seams. Pin, as shown, and machine-sew or backstitch all around the side edges using a 1-cm (⅜-in.) seam allowance. Place two of the arm pieces right sides together; pin and stitch all around using a 1-cm (⅜-in.) seam allowance and leaving a 6.5 cm (2½ in.) opening between the notches. Join the remaining arm and leg pieces together in the same way.

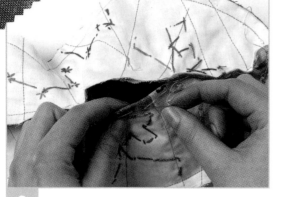

9 Along each edge of all of the openings, fold and press 6 mm (¼ in.) to the wrong side. Tack these turnings in place, as shown.

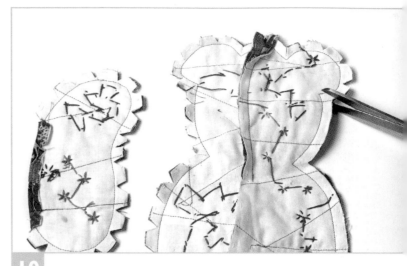

10 Snip notches close to the seam line along all of the curved edges, as shown. Around the ears, notch every 1 cm (⅜ in.); around gentler curves, the notches can be farther apart. At inner corners, such as under the chin, at each side of the ears, and at the ankles, snip into the corners, as shown.

11 Turn the patchwork body right side out. Push a small amount of polyester fibrefill into each ear, then machine-sew across the base of each ear, as shown.

12 Continue stuffing the bear, filling the head first, then the body. The filling should be firm. Push it in hard with your fingers, a little at a time, to prevent lumps. Slip-stitch the opening closed, as shown, using thread that blends with the patchwork. Fill the arms and legs and slip-stitch the openings in the same way.

13 Draw a circle with a 2.5-cm (1-in.) diameter around each joint dot. Match one circle on the body to the circle on the corresponding arm, arranging the arm at a suitable angle. Hold the pieces firmly together. With a double strand of cotton sewing thread in the sewing needle, slip-stitch the two circles together. Stitch all around the circles twice. Sew on the other limbs in the same way.

TIPS

■ At Step 13 you can choose to arrange the legs for the bear to sit or stand.

■ Embroidered eyes are recommended for bears for children under the age of three. Instead of sewing on buttons, work satin-stitch circles in black thread to match the nose.

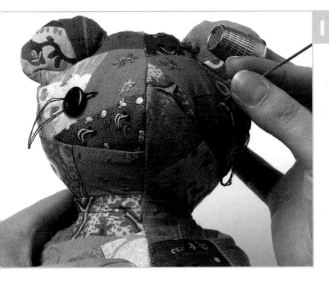

14 Thread the doll needle or large darning needle with doubled black cotton sewing thread and sew two black buttons at the eye dots, passing the needle right through the head from one eye to the other several times and pulling firmly to shape the head slightly. Bury the thread ends inside the head.

15 Use black pearl cotton No. 5 and the doll needle or darning needle to embroider the nose as a triangle of satin stitch, and add a smile in backstitch. Add a ribbon bow around the neck, stitching it in place with matching thread to keep it from coming undone.

Chapter 3

THE STITCH COLLECTION

Embroidering your crazy patchwork can transform a simple piece or add a final flourish to your work. You can embroider along some, or all, of your crazy-patchwork seams, sprinkle plain areas with detached stitches, or even add flowers and other motifs. Try out stitches on fabric scraps using different types of embroidery thread to see how versatile this art can be.

BLANKET STITCHES

As one of the most versatile stitches used in crazy patchwork, blanket stitch has many variations and several uses. You can use these stitches to decorate straight or curved seams, secure hand-pieced patches onto backing fabric, or work them in bands or circles to add extra decoration.

Basic Blanket Stitch

The lines of basic blanket stitch can be curved or straight and the spacing and stitch length varied to suit the design. On curved edges the stitches should be evenly fanned. At corners work three or more stitches into the same place.

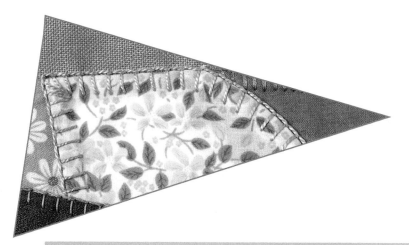

■ **1** Use an erasable fabric-marking pen to mark a line of evenly spaced dots parallel to a seam (or mark two parallel lines), between 6–12 mm (¼–½ in.) from the seam, with the dots spaced about 3–6 mm (⅛–¼ in.) apart. Working from left to right, bring the needle up at the left end of the lower line or seam at **a**. Form a loop with the thread and insert the needle at **b** on the upper line. Bring it out at **c**, directly below **b**, inside the loop. Pull through gently.

■ **2** Repeat to the right. Fasten down the last loop by making a small stitch along the lower line.

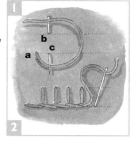

Closed Blanket Stitch

In this version of blanket stitch the "arms" are worked at angles, forming a line of triangles. Two lines worked back to back form little diamonds.

■ **1** Use an erasable fabric-marking pen to mark guidelines as for basic blanket stitch (above). Work from left to right. Bring the needle up at **a**, at the left end of the lower line, or the seam. Form a loop with the thread and insert the needle at **b**, to the right along the upper line. Bring the needle out at **c**, just to the right of **a**, inside the loop. Pull through gently.

■ **2** Form a second thread loop and insert the needle again at **b**, then bring it out at **d** along the lower line, inside the new thread loop. Repeat this pair of stitches to the right, inserting the needle next at **e**. Fasten off the last pair of stitches with a small stitch along the lower line.

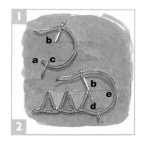

Long and Short Blanket Stitch

Simply by varying the length of the "arms" of the stitches, various decorative effects can be achieved. Two such lines of stitches can also be worked back to back.

■ Work from left to right, in the same way as for basic blanket stitch (opposite), but vary the length of the arms of the stitches as shown, in even steps. Each repeating group should consist of the same number of stitches – eight in the diagram.

Sloping Blanket Stitch

Blanket stitch can be worked with the "arms" sloping in either direction, and two such lines of stitches may be worked back to back.

■ **1** Use an erasable fabric-marking pen to mark guidelines as for blanket stitch (opposite). Work from left to right. Bring the needle up at **a**, at the left end of the lower line, or the seam. Form a loop with the thread and insert the needle at **b** on the upper line, directly above **a**. Bring it out at **c**, along the lower line to the right, inside the loop. Pull through. To make the next stitch, insert the needle at **d**, directly above **c**, and bring it out at **e**, as shown at right. Repeat to the right. Fasten down the last loop with a small stitch along the lower line. The stitch "arms" slope from top left to lower right.

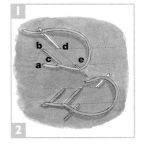

■ **2** For a slightly different effect, stitches may also be worked to slope in the opposite direction.

Crossed-Sloping Blanket Stitch

This stitch forms a bold line of crosses; it is suitable for decorating straight seam lines.

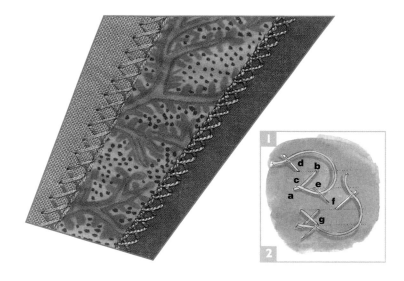

■ **1** Use an erasable fabric-marking pen to mark guidelines as for basic blanket stitch (see page 108). Work from left to right. Begin with a blanket stitch sloping from lower left to upper right (see Sloping Blanket Stitch, page 109): Bring the needle up at **a**, at the left end of the lower line or seam and form a loop with the thread. Take the needle down at **b**, along the upper line to the right. Bring it out again at **c**, just right of **a**, inside the loop. Pull through. Then work a stitch sloping in the other direction: Form a loop with the thread and insert the needle at **d**, directly above **c**, and bring it out at **e**, directly below **b**, inside the thread loop. Pull through.

■ **2** To begin the next stitch, form a loop and insert the needle at **f**. Bring it out at **g**, inside the new loop, but just outside the loop of the previous stitch. Continue to the right, fastening off the last loop with a small stitch along the lower line.

Loop Stitch

This stitch is closely related to the basic blanket stitch and forms a wide, spiky line that can be curved or straight. Worked along a patchwork seam, the knotted centre of the stitch should fall exactly on the seam. For an interesting effect, vary the length of the arms.

■ **1** Using an erasable fabric-marking pen, draw two guidelines, one on either side of a seam line and at a distance of 6 mm (¼ in.) or so from the seam, or simply draw three parallel guidelines. Work from right to left. Bring the needle up at **a**, at the right end of the centre line, or the seam. Insert the needle at **b** on the upper line and bring it out at **c** on the lower line. Pull through. Loop the thread as shown at left and pass the needle under the stitch between **a** and **b** without piercing the fabric, and inside the loop, as shown.

■ **2** Continue working to the left: Insert the needle at **d** and bring it out at **e**. Pull through, form a loop, and pass the needle under the previous stitch as before. Repeat as required. Fasten off with a small stitch on the centre line to hold the last loop in place.

Blanket-Stitch Wheels

Small circles of blanket stitch, with all the arms meeting at a central point, form little wheels that may be scattered across a patchwork, singly or in groups. Placing the meeting point off-centre makes a less formal effect, and partial circles resemble little shells or fans.

■ **1** Use an erasable fabric-marking pen to mark a circle on the fabric, with a dot for the centre point (the dot may be off-centre, if desired). Work anticlockwise, turning the work as stitching proceeds. Bring the needle up on the edge of the circle, form a loop with the thread, and insert the needle at the dot. Bring the needle up again a short distance along the edge, inside the loop, and pull through gently.

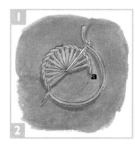

■ **2** Repeat around the circle, always inserting the needle at the same centre point. Form the last stitch by passing the needle under the first stitch (at **a**) without piercing the fabric and inserting the needle at the centre, as before.

TIP

To mark accurate circles for blanket-stitch wheels and flowers, try drawing around small objects, such as a thread spool or thimble. The centres, however, must be marked by eye. You can also purchase plastic stencils for circles of various sizes from office or art-supply stores.

Blanket-Stitch Flowers

Circles of blanket stitch may also be worked with the arms pointing outwards for a spiky effect, like little daisies. For a less formal look, make the arms alternately long and short, move the centre to one side, or work partial circles.

■ **1** Use an erasable fabric-marking pen to mark two circles on the fabric, one for the outer circle and a smaller one inside it, at the centre (or to one side). Work clockwise, turning the work as stitching proceeds. Bring the needle up at **a**, on the inner circle. Form a loop with the thread and insert the needle at **b** on the outer circle. Bring it out at **c**, just to the right of **a** on the inner circle, inside the loop of thread. Pull through gently.

■ **2** Repeat around the circle, spacing as required.

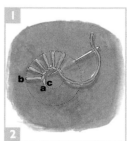

CHAIN STITCHES

Basic chain stitch is very easy to work, forming a slender line that curves gracefully. Some variations of it will form broader lines, suitable for edging patches or securing patchwork seams. Other stitches in this group form interesting knotted lines that can be used as borders or to form flowers and other motifs.

Basic Chain Stitch and Whipped Chain Stitch

Chain stitches form a slender, even line that can be straight or curved and used to emphasize a patchwork seam line or to add wavy lines to plain patches. Whipping a line of chain stitch with a contrasting thread colour makes it bolder and more ropelike.

■ **1** Use an erasable fabric-marking pen to mark the fabric with a series of regularly spaced dots in a straight or curved line, or use a fabric with an even pattern, such as gingham check, as a guide. Stitches should be 3–9 mm (⅛–⅜ in.) long. Work from top to bottom. Bring the needle up at **a**, and form a loop with the thread, then insert the needle again at **a** and bring it out at **b**, a short distance down the line, inside the loop of thread. Pull through.

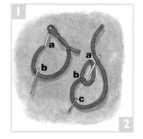

■ **2** Form another loop with the thread and insert the needle again at **b**, bringing it out at **c**, inside the loop. Pull through.

■ **3** Repeat the stitch as required. At the end of the line, finish off the last stitch by inserting the needle just outside the last loop.

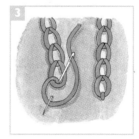

WHIPPED CHAIN STITCH

■ To whip a line of chain stitch, turn the work and stitch from right to left. Using a contrasting, heavier thread and a sharp needle, bring the thread up through the fabric from below the first chain, at **a**, then change to a blunt-tipped tapestry needle to avoid splitting the threads. Pass the needle from **b** to **c** under the next chain stitch without piercing the fabric. Do not pull too tightly. Repeat along the line. At the end, change to a sharp needle and pass it through the fabric underneath the last chain stitch.

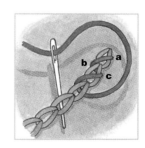

Open Chain Stitch

This variation on the basic chain stitch makes a wider line, suitable for decorating or for securing patchwork seams, whether they are straight or curved.

■ Use an erasable fabric-marking pen to mark the fabric with two parallel lines of dots, spaced about 6–9 mm (¼–⅜ in.) apart. Work from top to bottom. Bring the needle up at **a**, top left, and form a loop with the thread. Insert the needle at **b**, top right, bringing it out at **c**, a short distance down the left-hand line, inside the loop. Form another loop and insert the needle at **d**, a short distance down the right-hand line, opposite **c**. Bring the needle out at **e**, below **c** and inside the loop, to begin the next stitch. Repeat as required. Secure the last loop in a similar way to chain stitch (see page 112), but with two tiny stitches, one at each lower corner.

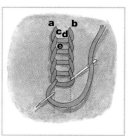

(see page 112)

TIP

With practice, stitches of equal length can be made by eye, avoiding the need to mark lines of dots.

Zigzag Chain Stitch

■ **1** Use an erasable fabric-marking pen to draw two parallel lines of dots on the fabric, placed alternately to left and right. The lines and dots should be about 6–9 mm (¼–⅜ in.) apart and may lie along one edge of a patch or on either side of a seam. Fabric with a small check can provide an instant guide. Bring the needle up at **a**, and make a chain stitch as opposite, bringing the needle out at **b** on the opposite line.

■ **2** Make a second chain stitch sloping back to the left. Repeat these two stitches as required. Fasten off the last loop as for chain stitch.

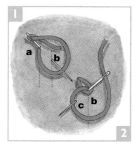

This simple variation on chain stitch is suitable for edging patches or securing patchwork seams. Alternatively, lines of zigzag chain stitch can be used to add interest to plain patches. It is easiest to work this stitch in straight lines.

Feathered Chain Stitch

This popular stitch makes a broad, decorative line that can be straight or curved. Use it to decorate patchwork seams or to secure patches onto backing fabric, either along the edge of a patch or spanning a seam line.

■ **1** Use an erasable fabric-marking pen to draw two parallel lines on the fabric, about 9–15 mm (⅜–⅝ in.) apart, or draw one line to one side of a seam. Work the line of stitches from top to bottom. Bring the needle up at **a**, top right. Form a loop with the thread and bring the needle out at **b**, inside the loop, below and to the left. Pull through.

■ **2** Make a straight stitch of a length to match the loop, inserting the needle at **c** and bringing it out on the left-hand line at **d**, level with **b**.

■ **3** Loop the thread and insert the needle again at **d**, bringing it out at **c**, inside the loop. Pull through.

■ **4** Make another straight stitch, inserting the needle at **e**. Bring it out again at **f**, level with **c**, to begin the next stitch. Repeat down the line. Fasten off the last loop with a straight stitch to match previous stitches.

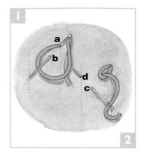

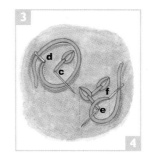

Double Chain Stitch

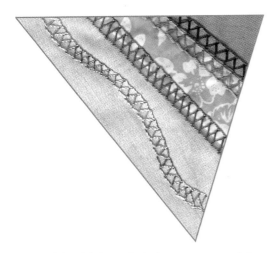

Use this broad stitch to secure straight or curved patches or to decorate seams. A line of double chain stitch may be placed on the edge of a patch or it can straddle a seam, and curved lines can add interest to plain areas.

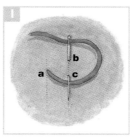

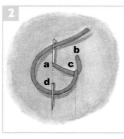

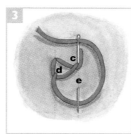

■ **1** Mark the fabric with two parallel lines of dots, 6–9 mm (¼–⅜ in.) apart, or one line parallel to a seam, using an erasable fabric-marking pen. A gingham check fabric can provide an instant guide. Work from top to bottom. Bring the needle up at **a**, on the left-hand line, form a loop with the thread and insert the needle at **b** on the right-hand line. Bring the needle out at **c**, on the right-hand line, inside the loop. Distances **a–b** and **a–c** should be equal. Pull through.

■ **2** Now form a second thread loop and insert the needle again at **a**, bringing it out at **d**, inside the loop. Pull through.

■ **3** Form a third thread loop and insert the needle again at **c**, bringing it out at **e** inside the loop. Pull through. Continue forming stitches to left and right to the end of the line, fastening off the last stitch in the same way as for chain stitch (see page 112).

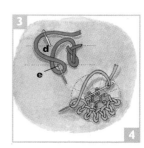

Scroll Stitch

Scroll stitch forms a flowing, knotted line, suitable for straight lines and bold curves. For best results, choose a rounded thread, such as pearl cotton.

■ **1** Use an erasable fabric-marking pen to mark the fabric with a line of dots, about 4–9 mm (³⁄₁₆–³⁄₈ in.) apart. Work from left to right. Bring the needle up at **a**, at the left end of the line. Form a clockwise loop of thread to the right, as shown at right, and insert the needle at **b**, inside the loop and just above the line. Bring it out at **c**, still inside the loop, but just below the line. Pull through gently and repeat to the right.

■ **2** Do not pull too tightly, but aim to make all of your knots the same size. Fasten off the last knot with a small stitch along the line.

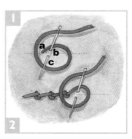

Double-Knot Stitch

This stitch makes a slender knotted line, which can be straight or gently curving. It may also be worked in a zigzag.

■ **1** Use an erasable fabric-marking pen to draw a line of equally spaced dots, about 4–9 mm (³⁄₁₆–³⁄₈ in.) apart. Work from left to right. Bring the needle up at **a**, the left end of the line, insert it at **b**, above the dotted line, bringing it out at **c**, just below. Pull through.

■ **2** Pass the needle under the first stitch from top to bottom as shown at right, without piercing the fabric. Pull through but do not tighten completely.

■ **3** Pass the needle under the first stitch again, to the right of the loop, with the thread beneath the needle tip as shown at right, and pull through. Repeat to the right. Take the thread to the back to fasten off.

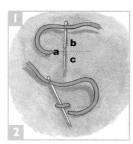

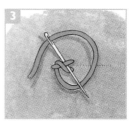

Rosette Chain

This decorative stitch can be used to secure patches or to embellish seams, and two lines worked back to back make a broad braid-like border. It may also be worked in a circle, as a small flower.

■ **1** Use an erasable fabric-marking pen to mark the fabric with two parallel lines about 6–9 mm (¼–³⁄₈ in.) apart, or one line parallel to a seam. Work from right to left. Bring the needle up at **a**. Form an anticlockwise loop with the thread as shown and insert the needle at **b**, about 6 mm (¼ in.) along the top line, bringing it out at **c** on the lower line, a little to the right and inside the thread loop. Pull through.

■ **2** Pass the needle upwards under the first part of the stitch without piercing the fabric.

■ **3** Loop the thread as before and insert the needle at **d**, bringing it out at **e** inside the loop to begin the next stitch. Pass the needle under the first part of this stitch and repeat to the left.

■ **4** To stitch a small flower, draw a circle with a radius of about 12 mm (½ in.), with another, smaller circle – with a radius of about 6 mm (¼ in.) – at its centre. Work rosette-chain stitch in a circle.

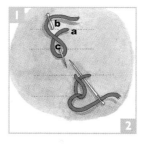

FEATHER STITCHES

The stitches in this group are traditionally used to decorate crazy-patchwork seams, both straight and curved. They may also be used to secure hand-pieced patches, avoiding the need to slip-stitch the patches in place. Some feather stitches may be worked closely together to fill leaf shapes or to form small motifs, such as the caterpillar on page 117.

Basic Feather Stitch

This quick and simple stitch makes a wide, spiky line, usually centred on a patchwork seam. The spacing and width of the stitches can be varied to suit the design.

■ **1** Use an erasable fabric-marking pen to draw a line on either side of a seam, each about 3–6 mm (⅛–¼ in.) from the seam, or simply draw three parallel guidelines. Work from top to bottom. Bring the needle up at **a**. Insert it at **b**, 3–6 mm (⅛–¼ in.) below, on the right-hand line. Bring the needle out at **c**, on the centre line, with the thread beneath the needle. Distance **a–b** should equal distance **b–c**. Pull through gently.

■ **2** Insert the needle at **d** on the left-hand line, and bring it out at **e** on the centre line, with the thread beneath the needle as before. Pull through.

■ **3** Repeat Steps 2 and 3 as required. Fasten down the last loop with a tiny stitch to hold it in place.

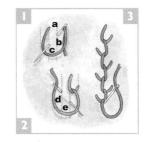

LONG-ARMED FEATHER STITCH

To stitch a long-armed version of this stitch, make sure the first insertion point, **b**, is higher than for basic feather stitch, and that point **d** is level with point **a**.

Double Feather Stitch

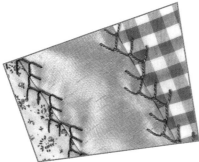

Widely used in traditional crazy patchwork, this airy, open version of feather stitch makes a wide zigzag line that can be either straight or gently curved.

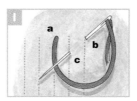

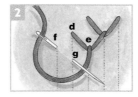

■ **1** Using an erasable fabric-marking pen, mark the fabric with two lines on either side of a seam, spaced up to 6 mm (¼ in.) apart, or draw five parallel lines. Work from top to bottom. Bring the needle up at the top of the centre line or seam at **a**. Form a loop with the thread and insert the needle at the top of the right-hand line at **b**, level with **a**. Bring the needle out again at **c**, midway between **a** and **b** and a short distance below.

■ **2** Make two more feather stitches down to the left: Insertion point **d** should be level with point **c**, and insertion point **f** (on the left-hand line) level with point **e**.

■ **3** Now make two feather stitches down to the right in the same way. Repeat Steps 2 and 3 as required. Fasten down the last loop with a small stitch in the same way as for feather stitch (above).

Open Cretan Stitch

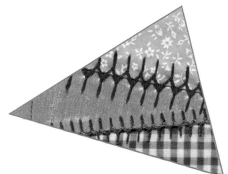

Open Cretan stitch is similar to feather stitch, but the spikes are worked at right angles to the line rather than sloping. Straight or curved lines of this stitch can be worked to cover the seams of crazy patchwork.

■ **1** Use an erasable fabric-marking pen to mark two lines on either side of the seam line, or simply mark four parallel lines. If the lines are 3 mm (⅛ in.) apart, the width of the embroidered line will be 9 mm (⅜ in). Work along the seam from left to right. Bring the needle up at **a**, and insert it at **b**, then bring it out again at **c**, directly below **b**, with the thread beneath the needle as shown. Pull through gently.

■ **2** Now insert the needle at **d** and bring it out at **e**, directly above **d**, again with the thread beneath the needle. Pull through. Repeat Steps 2 and 3 to the right, spacing the stitches evenly. To fasten off, make a tiny stitch over the last loop to hold it in place.

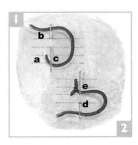

Cretan Stitch Variations

Curved and tapered lines, like this little caterpillar, can also be worked in Cretan stitch. For the caterpillar's eyes, use French knots (see page 125) or sew on tiny beads (see page 132). Small leaf shapes may be filled by working closely spaced Cretan stitch, giving a fernlike effect.

CURVED LINES

Draw four curved guidelines on the fabric using an erasable fabric-marking pen. Work as for ordinary open Cretan stitch (above), fanning the stitches evenly around the curves by making each stitch at a right angle to the lines.

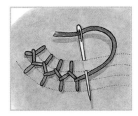

LEAF SHAPES

■ **1** Draw or trace a leaf outline onto the fabric using an erasable fabric-marking pen, and add a vein line down the centre. Work the leaf from top to bottom. Bring the needle up at **a**, at the top of the leaf. Insert it at **b** and bring it out at **c**, right of the centre line. Pull through gently.

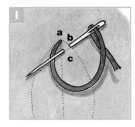

■ **2** Now insert the needle at **d** and bring it out at **e**, left of the centre line. Pull through.

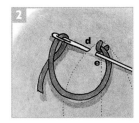

■ **3** Continue in this way, making stitches alternately to right and left until the shape is filled. The stitches may be almost horizontal or angled towards the base. To fasten off, hold down the last thread loop with a short stitch like a little stalk, as shown in the photograph.

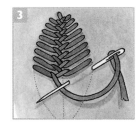

CROSSED STITCHES

The stitches in this group are traditionally used to decorate crazy-patchwork seams. They are best suited to straight seams because it is difficult to arrange them regularly around curves. Most of them may also be used to stitch down hand-pieced patches. Those that are worked singly rather than in lines may be scattered across the work in any formation.

Lines of Cross-stitch

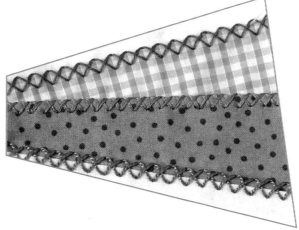

This simple stitch makes a firm, neat line, very suitable for securing patches. It may be worked along the edge of one patch or centred across a seam. A regular fabric pattern, such as a gingham check, can provide a ready-made guide for even stitches.

■ **1** Use an erasable fabric-marking pen to draw two parallel lines of evenly spaced dots, or one line to one side of a seam spacing the dots between 6–12 mm (¼–½ in.) apart. Begin by working a line of slanting stitches from right to left. Bring the needle up at **a**, at the right end of the lower line. Insert it at **b** on the upper line. Bring the needle out again at **c**, directly below **b** on the lower line. Pull through. Repeat to the left end of the line.

■ **2** Now work from left to right, completing each cross. Insert the needle at **d** on the upper line, and bring it out at **e** on the lower line. Pull through and repeat to the right.

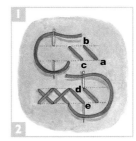

Single Cross-stitch

This is the familiar cross-stitch used in counted-thread embroidery. Each stitch is completed before moving on to the next. Evenly spaced stitches may be placed along one edge of a patch or centred over a seam. Stitches are also easily arranged to form simple step patterns. Note that the cross-stitch embroidery shown here was completed before patching.

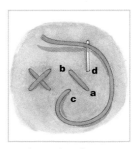

■ Use an erasable fabric-marking pen to mark lines of dots as above, or draw four dots for each individual cross-stitch. Work along a line from left to right. Bring the needle up at **a**. Insert it at **b**, upper left. Bring it out at **c**, lower left, and pull through. Insert the needle again at **d**, upper right, and pull through to complete the cross. Repeat as required. Note that the upper thread of the cross slants from lower left to top right: Make sure that the top threads of all the crosses slope in the same direction.

Tied Cross-stitch

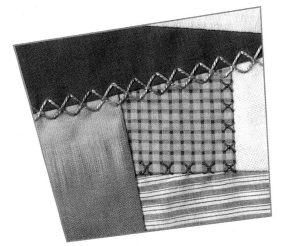

■ **1** Mark lines of dots on the fabric as for cross-stitch (opposite), using an erasable fabric-marking pen. Work lines from left to right, completing each stitch in turn. First, work a single cross-stitch as opposite, from **a** to **b**, then from **c** to **d**.

■ **2** Bring the needle up at **e**, close to the crossed threads, and take it down at **f**, tying the centre of the cross in place. Repeat as required.

This simple variation of cross-stitch may be worked quite large because the little tying stitches hold each cross firmly in place. Arrange the stitches in lines centred over a seam, or place them along the edges of a patch. Here, the gingham check fabric forms a guide for placing the stitches evenly.

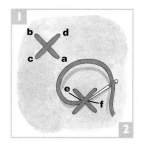

Herringbone Stitch

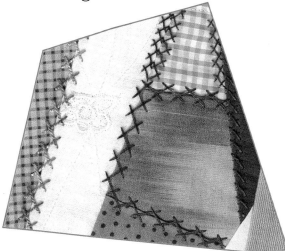

■ **1** Use an erasable fabric-marking pen to mark the fabric with two parallel lines, one on either side of a seam, or mark one line parallel to a seam. A spacing of 6–12 mm (¼–½ in.) between lines suits most projects. For accuracy, mark equally spaced dots along each line; if you need to turn a corner, begin marking at the corner. Work from left to right. Bring the needle up at **a**, at the left end of the lower line. Insert it at **b**, diagonally across on the upper line, and bring it out at **c**. Pull through.

■ **2** Insert the needle at **d** on the lower line and bring it out at **e**. Pull through. Note that **e** is directly below **b**, and **c** is directly above point **d** of the previous stitch, (although these proportions may be varied if desired). On a straight line of stitches, all of the sloping stitches should be parallel.

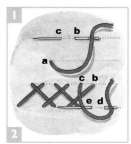

Use lines of herringbone stitch to secure and decorate straight patchwork seams. A line may be worked centrally across a seam or placed to one side. Two parallel lines will form a diamond, or trellis pattern. Care must be taken when turning corners, so plan the arrangement carefully.

Tied Herringbone Stitch

This is a simple variation on the basic herringbone stitch, which may be worked larger than herringbone stitch, because the tying stitches add extra security. You could work the tying stitches in a contrasting colour for added interest.

TIP

Herringbone stitch and laced herringbone stitch may both be used to secure a length of narrow ribbon or cord, as illustrated on page 123.

■ First, work a line of herringbone stitch (see page 119). Work the tying stitches from right to left along the line. Bring the needle up at **a**, at the top of the upper intersection, and down at **b**, just below it. Bring the needle up at **c**, below the lower intersection, and insert it at **d**, just above it. Repeat to the left. Note that the needle always comes up on the outside of the herringbone stitch and descends towards the inside of the line.

Laced Herringbone Stitch

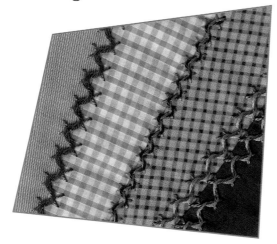

Adding lacing in a contrasting colour softens the spiky effect of a line of herringbone stitch and makes the line bolder. For a really dramatic effect, lace with a firm, rounded thread, such as pearl cotton Nos. 3 or 5, or soft embroidery cotton. Two lines worked parallel make a softly curving diamond pattern.

■ **1** First work a line of herringbone stitch (see page 119). Bring the lacing thread up at **a**, at the left end of the line, using a large, sharp needle, then change to a blunt-tipped tapestry needle to work the lacing. This will prevent catching the previous stitches. Without piercing the fabric, slip the needle up under the first arm and down under the second, forming a loop around the point where the stitches cross.

■ **2** Repeat to the right, as shown below. At the end of the line, change back to the sharp needle to take the lacing thread through to the wrong side of the work, inserting it at the end of the last arm.

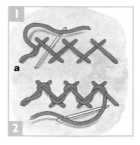

Ermine Stitch

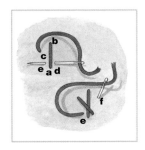

This decorative form of cross-stitch can be arranged in lines to secure or decorate seams, either across a seam or lengthways along it. Individual stitches may also be scattered across a patch. The proportions of this stitch can be varied, as desired.

■ Use an erasable fabric-marking pen to draw a line on either side of a seam, or simply draw three parallel lines. Mark dots along the seam or centre line at equal intervals, spaced up to 12 mm (½ in.) apart. Work in any convenient direction, completing each stitch in turn. Bring the needle up at **a**, and insert it at **b** directly above, forming a long vertical stitch. Make an elongated cross-stitch, from **c** to **d**, then from **e** to **f**. Points **c** and **f** should be about one-third of the stitch length down from **b** and the same distance to either side. Points **d** and **e** should be closer to point **a**. Stitches **c** to **d** and **e** to **f** should cross exactly over stitch **a** to **b**. Repeat as required.

Star Cross-stitch

Use this stitch to decorate and secure patchwork seams, or scatter single stars across a patch. Arrange the stitches in a continuous line, or space them as desired.

■ Use an erasable fabric-marking pen to draw a line on either side of a seam, each about 3–6 mm (⅛–¼ in.) from the seam, or simply draw three parallel lines. Each star is completed in turn, as shown below, but if working a line, work from left to right. First, work a single cross-stitch as on page 118, from **a** to **b**, then **c** to **d**. Bring the needle up at **e** and insert it at **f** directly above. Bring the needle up at **g** and pull through. Insert at **h**. Repeat as required.

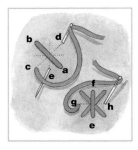

COUCHING STITCHES

Couching is the technique of embellishing the surface of the fabric with heavy threads, cords, braids or ribbons by stitching across them with a fine thread. The heavy thread or cord is called the "laid thread," and the fine thread the "tying thread." Heavy threads and cords may be couched in curved or straight lines, while ribbons and some braids are best used for straight lines only.

Plain Couching

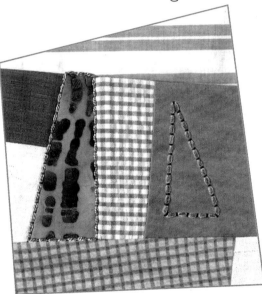

Plain couching may be used to edge a patch, or it can be laid along any seam line. The heavy laid thread can be one or two strands of pearl cotton, six strands of silk or cotton embroidery thread or any fine cord of a similar thickness. For the tying thread, use one or two strands of cotton embroidery thread, or any thread of an equivalent weight.

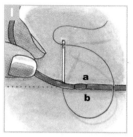

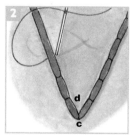

■ **1** Use an erasable fabric-marking pen to mark the fabric with a series of regularly spaced dots, about 3–9 mm (⅛–⅜ in.) apart, in a straight or curved line, or use fabric with an evenly printed pattern, such as gingham check, as a guide. Mount the fabric in an embroidery hoop and work from right to left. Lay the laid thread along the marked line of dots, leaving a 7.5-cm (3-in.) tail at the right end of the line. Tack it in place with the tying thread. Bring the needle and tying thread up at **a**, and make a small vertical stitch across the laid thread, inserting the needle at **b**. The tying thread should not pierce the laid thread. Repeat to the left at regular intervals, using the marked dots as a guide.

■ **2** When turning a sharp corner, the laid thread must be held with a stitch positioned exactly on the corner. Bring the tying thread up at **c** and insert it at **d**.

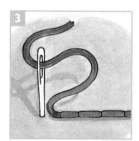

■ **3** When the couching is complete, leave the needle and tying thread on the wrong side of the fabric. Use a large darning needle to pass the tail of the laid thread through to the wrong side of the work.

■ **4** Fold the laid thread back along the line of stitching and use the tying thread to sew it to the backing fabric for about 2 cm (¾ in.); snip off the excess. Unpick the tacking at the beginning of the line and pass the first tail of laid thread through the fabric, using the darning needle. Use the thread from the tacking to secure the tail of laid thread to the backing fabric, as before.

Couched Motifs

Couching may also be used to add simple outline motifs to your crazy patchwork. Using a laid thread such as pearl cotton, tight curves and loops can be stitched easily.

■ Use an erasable fabric-marking pen to draw the desired outline on the fabric. Plan your stitching route around the outline. Work the outline in plain couching, as opposite. For tight curves, tying stitches should be placed about 3 mm (⅛ in.) apart.

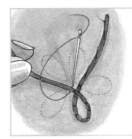

Zigzag Couching

This couching variation makes a broader, more decorative line than plain couching. It is suitable for embellishing or securing straight or curved patchwork seams. Two lines side by side can form parallel zigzags or a diamond pattern. Flat ribbon may also be attached in this way, in straight lines only.

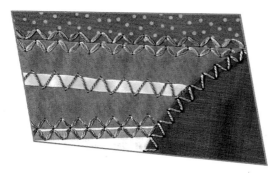

■ Use an erasable fabric-marking pen to draw a line to one side of the seam, about 6 mm (¼ in.) from the seam, or simply mark two parallel lines. Dots spaced 6–9 mm (¼–⅜ in.) apart in a zigzag formation can also be used. Work from right to left. Secure the laid thread on the surface as for plain couching (opposite) and bring the tying thread up at **a**, below the upper line and below the laid thread. Insert the needle at **b** on the upper line, over the laid thread, making a small vertical stitch. Hold the laid thread across the lower line and bring the needle up at **c**, then insert it at **d** on the lower line, over the laid thread. Repeat to the left. Secure the thread tails as for plain couching.

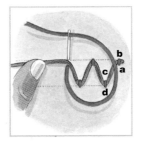

Couching with Other Embroidery Stitches

Many other embroidery stitches may be used to couch laid threads in place.

1 Turquoise ribbon couched with blanket stitch (see page 108).
2 Gold cord couched with chain stitch (see page 112).
3 White ribbon couched with herringbone stitch (see page 119).
4 Blue cord couched with single cross stitch (see page 118).

5 Turquoise knitting tape couched with chevron stitch (see page 129).
6 White ribbon couched with groups of three French knots with tails (see page 125).
7 Gold cord couched with fly stitch (see page 124).
8 Blue cord couched with feathered chain stitch (see page 114).

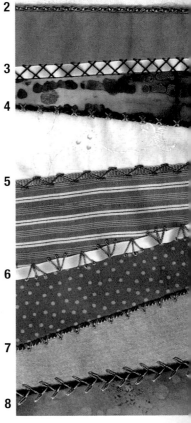

DETACHED STITCHES

These detached stitches add interest to crazy patchwork wherever it may be needed. Experiment with several different types of threads to create a variety of exciting embellishments.

Seeding Stitch

Pairs of small, straight stitches scattered across a plain area of patchwork can be used to add colour and texture to a dull area, improving the balance of the overall design. Vary the angles of the stitches randomly, and try to spread them evenly.

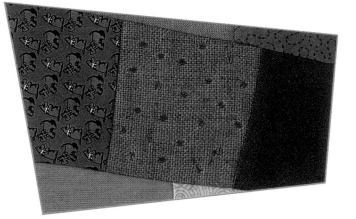

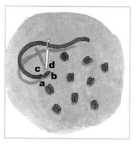

■ Use an erasable fabric-marking pen to mark the fabric with dots spaced about 12 mm (½ in) apart. At each dot, work a pair of stitches, varying the angle of each pair. Bring the needle up at **a**, and insert it at **b**, making a stitch 2–3 mm (½–⅛ in.) long. Then make another stitch next to the first, from **c** to **d**. Repeat as required.

Detached Chain Stitch

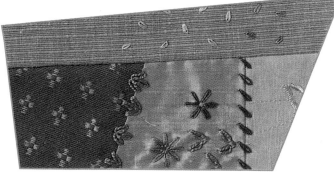

■ Mark the fabric with a series of small lines about 6–9 mm (¼–⅜ in.) long using an erasable fabric-marking pen. Bring the needle up at **a**, and form a loop with the thread. Insert the needle again at **a**, and bring it out at **b**, inside the loop. Pull through. Insert the needle at **c**, just outside the loop, and pull through to secure the chain. Repeat as required. To add a little tail, point **c** may be a short distance below **b**.

Sometimes called lazy daisy stitch, or single chain, this stitch can be arranged in groups to make flowers with five to eight petals (often with a French knot at the centre, as opposite). Other arrangements can also be made – such as little groups of three stitches, shown here along a seam line – or detached chains can simply be sprinkled as desired.

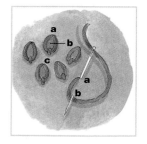

Detached Fly Stitch and Wheatear Stitch

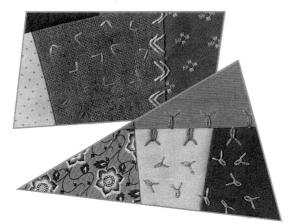

■ **1** Use an erasable fabric-marking pen to draw small V-shaped marks on the fabric. Space these regularly along seams or scatter them as desired. For each detached fly stitch, bring the needle up at **a**. Form a loop with the thread and insert the needle at **b**, bringing it out again at **c**, inside the loop. Pull through. Insert the needle at **d**, outside the loop, just below **c**. For a longer tail, point **d** may be some distance below **c**. Repeat as desired.

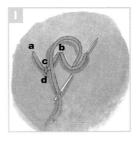

This simple stitch may be scattered across a plain patch or arranged along seam lines in various ways. The final holding stitch can also be lengthened to form a tail. You can finish with a chain stitch, instead of a straight holding stitch, to make a wheatear stitch.

WHEATEAR STITCH

■ **2** To turn a fly stitch into a wheatear stitch, form the fly stitch from **a** to **b** to **c**, as above; then instead of finishing with a straight stitch, work a chain stitch from **c** to **d** to **e**, as shown opposite.

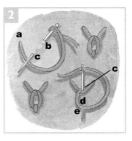

French Knots and French Knots with Tails

This well-known stitch can be scattered across a patch, evenly or at random, while lines of knots may be used to secure patchwork seams or ribbons. By lengthening the final stitch, a French knot with a tail is created, and these may be grouped in various ways to form flowers and other motifs.

■ **1** Mark the fabric with dots where desired, using an erasable fabric-marking pen. Mount the fabric in an embroidery hoop. Bring the needle up at **a**, and hold the thread taut. Wind the thread twice around the tip of the needle.

■ **2** Keeping the thread taut, insert the needle tip very close to **a** and pull it through to the wrong side. The twists should lie neatly on the fabric.

FRENCH KNOTS WITH TAILS

■ For a French knot with a tail, form the knot as above, but insert the needle at **b**, 3–6mm (⅛–¼ in) away from **a**. The knot will form at **b**.

TIP

To form a larger French knot, use heavier thread rather than winding the thread more than twice around the needle, which makes it more likely to tangle as you pull it through.

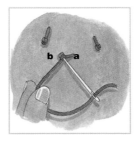

Star Stitch

Scatter these little stars across plain patches to add interest where desired, or work a single star where three or four patches meet. They are very quick and easy to work.

TIPS

■ When working star stitch, you can vary the number of radiating stitches, as desired, but remember that more than about ten will mean that the stitch will not lie flat at the centre.
■ You can also vary star stitch, by placing point **b** off centre.

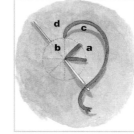

■ Use an erasable fabric-marking pen to draw a circle with a radius of about 6–9 mm (¼–⅜ in.) onto the fabric. Mark a dot at the centre and six or eight radiating lines. Bring the needle up at **a**, on the edge of the circle and insert it at **b**, the centre. Bring it out at **c** and insert it again at **b**. Continue around the circle, always bringing the needle out on the edge of the circle and inserting it at the centre. On loosely woven fabrics, a small eyelet hole will form at **b**.

Bullion Knots

This stitch forms a tight coil, groups of which can be arranged to make little stars or roses with a raised three-dimensional effect. Some practice is required to make neat stitches, and remember that if the coils are wound too tightly, it will be difficult to pull the needle through them.

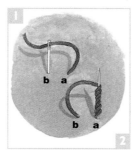

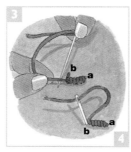

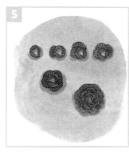

■ **1** For each bullion knot, mark the fabric with a line about 6–9 mm (¼–⅜ in.) long, using an erasable fabric-marking pen. Hold the work in an embroidery hoop. Use a needle that is slightly larger than you would normally choose for your particular thread. Bring the needle up at **a**, and insert it at **b**. Pull through, leaving a long loop on the surface.

■ **2** Bring the needle tip up again at **a**, and wind the thread around it anticlockwise, five to eight times (the number of turns depends on the weight of the thread and length of the stitch). Do not wind too tightly. Hold the twists in place with your left thumb and forefinger, and pull the needle through.

■ **3** Hold the thread down towards **b** and use the needle tip to pack the coils neatly, stroking them into place.

■ **4** Insert the needle at **b** and pull through to the wrong side.

■ **5** To make a rose, begin with a triangle of three bullion knots at the centre, then work a fourth knot around one corner – adding an extra coil will help it to curl. Continue adding more overlapping bullion knots, as desired.

Eyelet Wheels

Use this stitch to form small circular flowers, arranged along a seam or scattered, as desired. A partial circle may be added to the corner of a patch, making a fan shape.

■ **1** Use an erasable fabric-marking pen to draw a circle with a radius of about 6–9mm (¼–⅜ in.), a centre point, and about six or eight radiating lines onto the fabric. Bring the needle up at **a**, on the edge of the circle, and make a backstitch, inserting it at **b**, on the edge of the circle. Bring the needle out again at **a**, and insert it at **c**, the centre. Bring it out at **d** and make the next pair of stitches from **d** to **a**, then from **d** to **c**, bringing the needle out at **e** to begin the next repeat. On loosely woven fabrics a small eyelet hole will form at the centre.

■ **2** Point **c** may be placed off centre for a less formal effect.

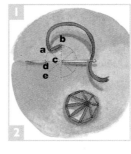

Detached Stitch Combinations

Detached stitches may be combined in various ways, not only to make little flowers and stars but also little insects, such as spiders, flies and moths. These are often found on traditional crazy-patchwork pieces, perhaps because of the damage such insects can cause to fabric – a tongue-in-cheek warning to the insect world!

The spider's web is couched in fine thread. First make radiating long stitches for the spokes, then plain couch (see page 122) a spiral from the centre outwards, working tying stitches over both the spiral and the spokes where they cross.

The spider's body is made from two detached chain stitches (see page 124), with two French knots for the head (see page 125) and eight backstitch legs (see page 128).

The green flies are formed using three detached chain stitches with a French knot for the head.

The pale moth has a bullion knot (see opposite) body, two French knots for the head and four detached chain stitches for wings.

LINE STITCHES

The stitches in this group have various uses. Plain backstitch, whipped backstitch and stem stitch form slender lines that are not really suitable for securing patchwork seams, but may be used as decoration in various ways. Threaded backstitches and chevron stitch form wider, more decorative lines that may be used to edge patches.

Backstitch, Whipped and Threaded Backstitch

This is the same backstitch that is used for seams (see page 21). The stitches form a slim, even line that may be straight or gently curved. Use this stitch to add contrast stripes to a plain patch, or for wavy lines, such as flower stems. Whipping a line of backstitch with a second thread makes a bolder, more interesting line.

■ **1** Use an erasable fabric-marking pen to mark the fabric with a straight or curved line. Work from right to left. Bring the needle up at **a**, and insert it a short distance to the right at **b**, bringing it out again along the line at **c**. The distance from **a–b** should equal **a–c**. Repeat to the left, inserting the needle next at **a**. Take care to make all stitches the same length—about 3–6 mm (⅛–¼ in.) will suit most projects.

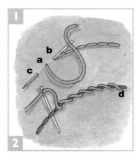

WHIPPED BACKSTITCH

■ **2** To whip the stitches, use a contrasting, heavier thread. Use a sharp needle to bring the thread up at **d**, from below the centre of the first backstitch; change to a blunt-tipped tapestry needle to avoid splitting the backstitches. Pass the needle under each backstitch in turn from top to bottom, without piercing the fabric or the stitch. At the end of the line, change to the sharp needle and insert it through the fabric at the centre of the last backstitch, just above the thread.

THREADED BACKSTITCH

■ **1** To thread a line of backstitch, begin in the same way as whipped backstitch (see above), but pass the blunt-tipped needle up and down under the backstitches, along the line from right to left.

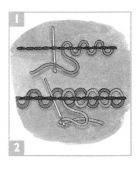

■ **2** A second thread may be added in the same way, making a double threaded line.

Chevron Stitch

Use this stitch to secure straight-edged patches. A single line of chevron stitches may straddle a patchwork seam, or be placed to one side. Two parallel lines may be worked to form a trellis or a zigzag pattern. Chevron stitch may also be used to couch down a ribbon, as on page 122.

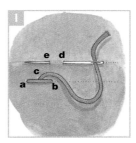

■ **1** Use an erasable fabric-marking pen to mark the fabric with a line on either side of, or parallel to, the seam. Work from left to right. Bring the needle up at **a**, on the lower line and make a small stitch to the right, inserting the needle at **b** and bringing it up at **c**, halfway along the stitch and above the thread. Insert the needle at **d** on the upper line and bring it out at **e**, directly above **b**.

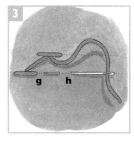

■ **2** Make a small stitch to the right, inserting the needle at **f** and bringing it out at **d**, below the thread.

■ **3** Insert the needle at **g** on the lower line and bring it out at **h**, directly below **f**. Repeat to the right.

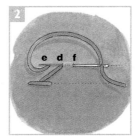

Stem Stitch

This stitch forms a narrow, smooth, unbroken line that winds easily around curves, making it suitable for flower stems and other decorations. Choose a stitch length to suit the weight of your thread and the tightness of the curve required: The tighter the curve, the smaller your stitches should be.

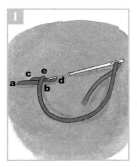

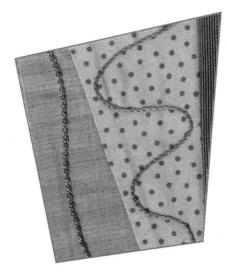

■ **1** Use an erasable fabric-marking pen to mark the fabric with a straight or smoothly curving line. Work from left to right. Bring the needle up at **a**, at the left end of the line. Insert the needle at **b**, 3–6 mm (⅛–¼ in.) along the line and bring it out again at **c** just above the first stitch, halfway along it. Pull through. Insert the needle at **d** and bring it out again at **e**, above the thread of the previous stitch. Repeat to the right.

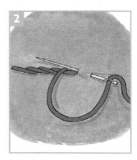

■ **2** To make a broader line, make the stitches at a slight angle. Insert the needle on the lower edge of the marked line and bring it out on the upper edge, always above the previous stitch, as before.

SATIN STITCHES

Satin stitches are used to fill small areas with closely packed stitches, forming a smooth surface. They are suitable for working small motifs, such as flowers and leaves. Cotton or silk embroidery thread is the best choice of thread for these stitches; using two or three strands together will give a flat, glossy appearance.

Straight and Slanted Satin Stitch

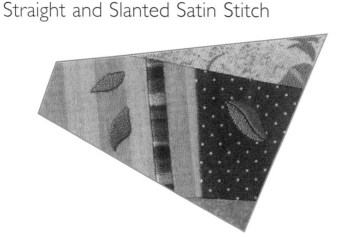

Leaves, petals and other small motifs can be added to crazy patchwork using satin stitch. Worked in cotton or silk embroidery thread, the glossy surface will produce a play of light and shadow across different sections of the design. You can also use satin stitch to highlight details of a printed fabric.

■ **1** Draw an outline of the area to be covered with an erasable fabric-marking pen. Bring the needle up at **a**, at the lower left of the area and insert it at **b** along the straight grain of the fabric. Bring the needle out at **c**, one fabric thread to the right of **a**, and insert it at **d**, one fabric thread to the right of **b**. Bring the needle out at **e** to continue stitching to the right.

SLANTED SATIN STITCH

■ **2** Begin at the centre of the shape, bringing the needle up at **a**, and inserting it at **b**. Repeat to the right. Pass the needle through the backs of the stitches, back to the centre, and work more parallel stitches out from the centre to the left.

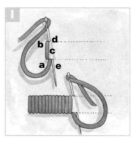 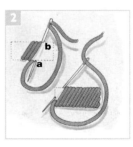

Padded Satin Stitch

Padding a satin-stitch motif gives an embossed effect. Care must be taken to completely cover the padding with stitches.

■ **1** For the padding use colourfast felt or craft interfacing; if possible, choose a colour to blend with the thread. Cut the required shape from the padding and stitch the shape in place with matching thread and tiny stitches. (Iron-on craft interfacing may also be used and this stitching omitted.)

■ **2** Cover the shape with slanted satin stitch as above.

■ **3** Details, such as leaf veins, may be added in backstitch, working through all the layers of padding and fabric together.

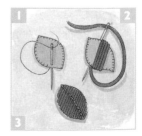

Long and Short Satin Stitch

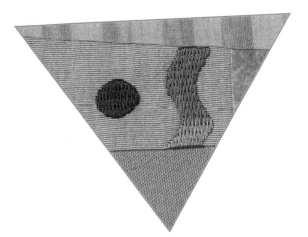

This satin-stitch variation is used for somewhat larger areas, where satin stitches would be too long to be stable. Several rows of long and short stitches are worked to fill the area completely. These rows may be all the same colour or worked in different hues for a shaded effect.

■ **1** Mark the design outline on the fabric, using an erasable fabric-marking pen. It is a good idea to divide the area with several parallel guidelines, no more than 6 mm (¼ in.) apart. Begin at top left of the shape. Bring the needle up at **a**, and insert it at **b** on the top edge, making a short stitch. Then bring the needle up at **c** and insert it at **d**, making a long stitch. Repeat to the right. On this top row, all the stitches end at the top edge.

■ **2** On subsequent rows bring the needle up at **e** and insert it at **f**, piercing the base of the stitch above. Then bring the needle up at **g** and insert it at **h**, again piercing the stitch above. All of the stitches in this row are the same length. At the lower edge of the shape, all stitches will begin at the lower edge and end in the base of the stitches above, so they will be alternately long and short.

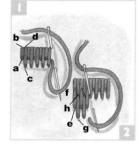

Shaded Satin Stitch

For flower petals and leaves and other tapering, irregular shapes, long-and-short stitches may be fanned out to suit the shape. Working the rows of stitches in different colours of thread makes a realistic effect: Three close colours often work well.

■ **1** Draw or transfer the required outline as for satin stitch (opposite). Divide the area with several parallel guidelines. Begin at the centre of the outside edge and work a row of long and short satin stitches, as above, out to the right, then return to the centre and work out to the left. The stitches should not be parallel to each other, but point towards the centre of the lower line. They must be close enough to cover the fabric completely along the top edge.

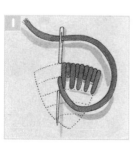

■ **2** With another shade of thread, work the next row of stitches, fitting them between the stitches above. These stitches should all be the same length. If the shape tapers sharply, miss some stitches. Repeat this row as required, perhaps in a third shade of thread.

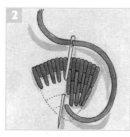

■ **3** At the lower edge, make long and short stitches, as required, to cover the shape. Make sure that no fabric is visible between the stitches.

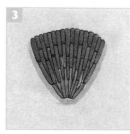

SEQUINS AND BEADS

Some easy ways to sew on beads, sequin, and charms are shown on page 84, but you may enjoy the following special stitches and techniques as well.

Lines of Sequins

When attaching solid lines of sequins, whether straight or curved, you can choose whether the stitches should be visible or invisible. For the invisible method, the sequins overlap, so more of them are required.

VISIBLE STITCHES

■ **1** Use an erasable fabric-marking pen to draw a guideline on the fabric or follow a patchwork seam. For the visible stitch method, a contrasting thread is often used. Work from right to left. Bring the needle up at **a**, and thread a sequin onto the needle. Hold the sequin flat on the fabric and make a backstitch (see page 128) to the right, inserting the needle at **b**, on the edge of the sequin. Bring the needle up again at **c** to attach the next sequin to the left. Repeat as required to cover the marked line.

INVISIBLE STITCHES

■ **2** For the invisible stitch method, use a thread colour that blends with the sequins. Work from right to left. Bring the needle up at **a**, and place the sequin with its left edge at **a**. Insert the needle through the sequin and the fabric at **b**. Bring the needle out again at **c** to attach the next sequin. Hold the sequin with its left edge at **c** and insert the needle through the sequin and the fabric, just on the edge of the previous sequin. The sequins overlap and no stitches can be seen.

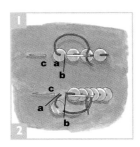

Bead and Sequin Motifs

Little flower motifs are simple to stitch with beads or sequins. Sequins may be stitched in place using tiny beads, as on page 84, or in lines or circles, as above. Lines and circles of beads may also be couched, as shown here.

■ A string of beads may be couched in place with a second thread. Work from right to left. Use a strong thread to hold the beads: Bring the needle up at **a**, and thread on the required beads. Leave this needle "parked" in the fabric to the left. Thread a second needle with a finer thread and bring it up at **b**, above the bead thread, then insert it at **c**, below the bead thread, making a tiny stitch over the bead thread, between two beads. Repeat to the left, making a tying stitch between each pair of beads. When couching is complete, pass the first needle and the bead thread through to the wrong side of the fabric and fasten it off securely.

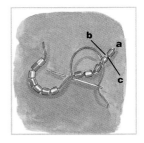

Shisha Stitch

Shisha mirrors with ready-made borders are shown on page 85, but you can also attach the mirrors using the traditional Indian shisha stitch. A smooth, rounded thread, such as coton à broder or pearl cotton No. 8, shows the intricate border stitch to advantage. You can also add extra embroidery stitches around the shisha, like these French knots with tails (see page 125).

■ **1** Hold the mirror in place where required and bring the needle up at **a**, on the edge of the disk. Make a stitch across the mirror to **b**, then another from **c** to **d**. Bring the needle up at **e**, slip it beneath the first stitch as shown, then beneath the second in the same way, and insert it at **f**.

■ **2** Bring the needle out again at **g**. Slip the needle beneath the second and first stitches, as shown and insert it at **h**. Keep stitches tight to hold the mirror in place.

■ **3** Bring the needle out again at **i**. Pass it beneath the first intersection as shown.

■ **4** Work clockwise around the edge. Form a loop with the thread and insert the needle again at **i**, bringing it out at **j**, inside the loop. Pull through, forming an open chain stitch (see page 113).

■ **5** Pass the needle under the single holding stitch as shown, and pull through.

■ **6** Form a loop with the thread, insert the needle again at **j** and bring it out at **k**, inside the loop, forming another open chain stitch. Repeat all around, passing the needle under both threads at the intersections of the holding stitches. Fasten off with a tiny stitch to hold the last open chain stitch in place.

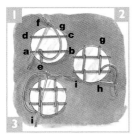
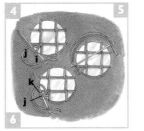

Adding Beads to Embroidery Stitches

Small beads can be added to embroidery stitches as you work them. You will need to choose a needle to fit through the beads; so heavy threads are not suitable for tiny seed beads.

1 Line of fly stitch (see page 125) with green beads. Work a line of fly stitches side by side, but before making the final holding stitch on each fly, thread a bead onto the needle.
2 Wheatear stitch with green beads. Work the wheatear variation of fly stitch shown on page 125, but before the final needle insertion, thread a bead onto the needle.
3 Sequins attached with detached chain stitches (see page 124) with long tails. Add a sequin to the holding stitch of each chain, lengthening these stitches to suit the size of the sequins.

TIPS

■ To use beads or loose sequins, tip them out into a small saucer and pick them up with the needle tip, as required. Keep a pair of tweezers handy for awkward pickups.
■ Choose a needle that fits easily through the holes in beads or sequins, then choose a weight of thread to suit the needle.
■ Never force a needle that is too large through a bead, because it will probably break it. Change to a smaller needle or try another bead: Hole sizes may vary slightly.

MACHINE-EMBROIDERY STITCHES

Machine-embroidery stitches can be used to decorate crazy-patchwork seams or to create motifs. In addition to patterns made by combining straight and zigzag stitches, there are many other ways to embellish your patchwork using a sewing machine. Whether you own a basic machine with a choice of utility stitches, a medium-range machine with preprogrammed embroidery stitches, or a top-of-the-line machine with computerized embroidery options, you will need to read the manufacturer's manual and make test samples in order to try out different stitches and threads.

Straight Stitch and Topstitch Motifs

Motifs such as these stars can be worked in straight stitch on any sewing machine. Automatic topstitch, available on some machines, allows you to sew each stitch three times (forwards, backwards, then forwards again), making a bold line.

■ **1** Use an erasable fabric-marking pen to draw the motif outline onto the fabric. Plan your stitching route around the outline: if you begin this star design at an inner corner (**a**), you can stitch all around without cutting the thread and starting again. Insert the work in a machine embroidery hoop or back it with stabilizer (see page 17), and stitch slowly, lifting the presser foot to reposition the work as necessary. Fasten off the thread tails on the wrong side of the fabric, as on page 27.

■ **2** For extra emphasis, you can stitch all around the motif twice (or even three times), using the same or contrasting colours of thread.

TOPSTITCH
■ **3** If your machine has an automatic topstitch setting, you can stitch a bolder line in a single colour. On corners or tight curves, stop at the end of a complete three-part stitch, with the needle down, then lift the presser foot and turn the work to avoid a ragged line.

Gimping

Cords, narrow ribbons and knitting yarns can be gimped onto a fabric surface using a machine zigzag stitch. Like couching by hand (see page 122), the stitches do not pierce the cord, but hold it flat to the fabric. Use cord for straight or curved lines or small motifs like this heart. Ribbons are best applied in straight lines.

■ **1** Leaving a 10-cm (4-in.) tail at the start, pin the cord carefully in place along the required line. Cut the cord, leaving another 10-cm (4-in.) tail. Set the machine for medium-length zigzag stitch, of a width to span the cord.

■ **2** Position the work under the needle so that it will pierce the fabric to the left or right of the cord. Stitch very slowly, piercing the fabric on either side of the cord and stopping with the needle down at the inside of curves and corners to turn the work.

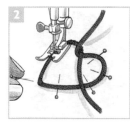

■ **3** Thread each cord tail into a darning needle and pass them through to the wrong side of the fabric.

■ **4** Use the sewing thread tails and a small sewing needle to stitch the tails down along the back of the gimped line for about 2.5 cm (1 in.), snipping off the excess.

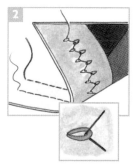

Twin Needle Stitching

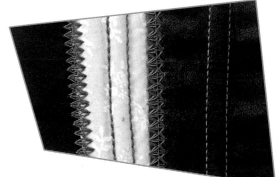

Stitching with a twin needle using two upper threads at the same time forms two parallel lines suitable for decorating straight seams or adding stripes to patches. You can choose straight stitch or topstitch (opposite), but the lines must be straight. The bobbin thread makes an interesting pattern, linking the two lines of stitches.

■ **1** If your sewing machine has only one thread spindle, wind a bobbin with the second thread and place it on the spindle together with the first spool. Thread the right needle eye with the thread from the lower (or right-hand) spool and the left with the thread from the upper (or left-hand) spool or extra bobbin. Follow straight patchwork seams as a guide, or stitch in a straight line. Topstitch (see opposite) makes bolder lines than straight stitch.

REVERSE PATTERN

■ **2** Choose a bobbin thread colour, and one or two contrasting colours for the two upper threads. Loosen the thread tension so that the upper threads are pulled through the fabric in loops by the tighter bobbin thread. Turn the work over. Follow a patchwork seam as a guide, or draw a guideline on the fabric using an erasable fabric-marking pen. Stitch with the wrong side uppermost, using straight stitch, or topstitch (opposite) for a denser pattern.

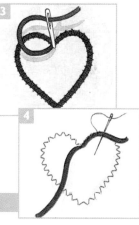

Bobbin Thread Zigzag

Threads that are too heavy for use as upper machine threads can be wound onto a bobbin and applied to the fabric surface by stitching from the wrong side. Various widths and lengths of zigzag stitch can be used to decorate patchwork seams or to form little motifs such as the spiral shown here.

■ **1** Wind a heavy thread (such as coton à broder or pearl cotton Nos 5 or 8) by hand onto a spare bobbin. Make sure you wind in the same direction as the machine-wound process. Insert the bobbin and choose a matching or contrasting colour for the upper sewing thread. Set the sewing machine for zigzag stitch and loosen the upper thread tension by one or two settings.

■ **2** Turn the work over. Follow a patchwork seam as a guide, or draw guidelines on the wrong side of the fabric with an erasable fabric-marking pen. Stitch slowly with the wrong side uppermost. Further loosening of the upper thread tension causes the heavy thread to pull little loops of the sewing thread through the fabric, making a spiky line. Experiment with different heavy threads, stitch lengths, stitch widths and tension settings, to produce a variety of looped and spiky lines.

Free-Motion Stippling

Use this technique to fill a patch with a random looped line of stitches. This treatment is useful for altering the visual balance of coloured patches. For example, stippling a patch with a colour similar to the surrounding patches, as here, evens out the balance of colours, while stitching in a contrasting colour will add interest to a dull patch.

■ **1** Set the sewing machine for free-motion stitching; the fabric movement will be controlled by your hands, not by the machine, and there must be no pressure from a presser foot. Machine models differ, but try these tricks:

Disengage the feed dogs (the serrated moving tracks in the throat plate). Some machines have a control to lower the feed dogs out of action; otherwise, cover the feed dogs with a piece of thin card or plastic taped in place.

Set the stitch length to zero.

Use a darning (stippling) foot. This has a large hole, and the foot itself is made from transparent plastic, so you can see the stitches below it.

Alternatively, remove the presser foot and use a spring needle. To stitch, you must still lower the presser-foot assembly to engage the thread tension. Keep your fingers away from the unprotected needle when stitching.

■ **2** Use an erasable fabric-marking pen to draw a continuous curved line to fill the required area evenly, starting and ending at a seam line.

■ **3** Mount the work in a machine embroidery hoop. Set the thread tension as you would for straight stitching. Lower the needle by hand carefully at the beginning of the marked line and stitch very slowly, holding the hoop by the edges and moving it gently beneath the needle so that small stitches follow the guideline. With a little practice you can form even stitches in smooth curves.

Automatic Embroidery Stitches

1 Satin stitch blocks in pink 100 per cent cotton sewing thread.

2 Faux blanket stitch in orange viscose thread.

3 Satin stitch waves in gold metallic thread.

4 Satin stitch hearts in pink 100 per cent cotton sewing thread.

5 Faux feather stitch in pink viscose thread.

6 Little stars in gold metallic thread.

7 Little flowers in orange viscose thread.

8 Faux cross stitch in pink viscose thread.

Some sewing machines have an automatic embroidery capability, enabling you to stitch a variety of patterns. Follow the instructions in your owner's manual and always make a test piece before embroidering your project. It is a good idea to try out all of the stitches your machine is capable of, using different thread types and width/length settings, keeping a notebook of successful settings for future reference.

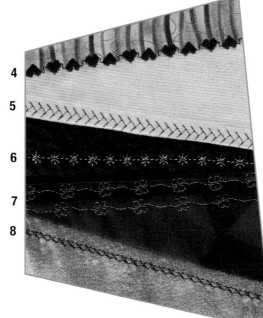

Computerized Embroidery

Top-of-the-range sewing machines can often automatically stitch computerized designs from a computer disk or by linking the machine directly to a computer. A wide variety of designs is available on disk or via the Internet, and you can learn to program your own designs. Consult the manual for your machine.

TIPS

■ Use 100 per cent cotton sewing thread for embroidery on articles that may require frequent laundering. Topstitching thread, which is stronger and heavier, is also suitable.

■ For more decorative articles, try speciality machine embroidery threads – such as viscose, metallic, or silk – in plain or shaded colours (see page 14).

■ For embroidering with special threads, especially on fine fabrics, choose a machine embroidery needle.

■ For all but the heaviest fabric, always use a machine-embroidery hoop (see page 15), stabilizer (see page 17), or water-soluble paper (see page 17).

Chapter 4

THE FABRIC DIRECTORY

There is a bewildering array of fabrics available to the modern sewing enthusiast, so in order to help you choose suitable types of fabric for your crazy-patchwork projects, the following directory includes basic fabrics – such as plain and printed cottons – suitable for most projects, together with examples of more specialized fabrics that you might wish to include in your work – such as velvet and lace.

PLAIN FABRICS

The backbone of your fabric stash should be a selection of plain fabrics in your choice of colours. Lightweight cottons are inexpensive and widely available in a huge range of colours, while linens, wools and silks have their own individual textures and qualities.

PLAIN COTTON

For crazy-patchwork backing fabric, white cotton fabric similar to sheeting is a good choice for most projects. Similar fabrics are available in a range of colours and weights. Plain cottons launder well.
Ease of use: Easy.
Weight: Light or medium.

COTTON CHAMBRAY

A fine, plain weave with a white warp and coloured weft. Launders well.
Ease of use: Easy.
Weight: Light.

COTTON DENIM

A tough and durable twill weave, traditionally with a white warp and blue weft.
Ease of use: Use with caution. Denim may not be colourfast, so pre-worn denim is often a useful choice.
Weight: Medium.
Avoid: Stretch or heavyweight denim.

SHOT COTTON

A plain weave with contrasting colours for warp and weft, shot cotton launders well and is available in a wide range of colour combinations.
Ease of use: Easy.
Weight: Light.

CORDED COTTON

A tightly woven, tough, durable fabric with a corded appearance.
Ease of use: Use with caution.
Weight: Medium.
Avoid: Heavyweight corded cotton.

LIGHTWEIGHT CORDUROY

Woven with fine stripes of "pile," lightweight corduroy adds a pleasing change of texture to any medium-weight project.
Ease of use: Easy.
Weight: Medium.
Avoid: Heavyweight corduroy.

COARSE-WEAVE LINEN

Coarse-weave linen is durable but creases easily. Pure linen and linen blends are available in a wide range of colours and weights.
Ease of use: Easy.
Weight: Light to medium.

MATKA SILK

A durable coarse-woven matt silk available in a wide range of colours. Frays easily.
Ease of use: Easy.
Weight: Medium.

WOOLLEN WEAVES

Woven wool fabrics are available in a wide range of textures and weights but often require careful laundering to avoid shrinkage.
Ease of use: Use with caution due to possible shrinkage.
Weight: Light to medium.
Avoid: Heavyweight and knitted (stretch) types.

NATURAL LINEN

Natural linen is durable but creases easily. Undyed linen is the natural colour of the flax that is used in its manufacture.
Ease of use: Easy.
Weight: Light to medium.

LINEN SLUB

Durable but creases easily. The texture is formed by weaving with threads of varying thickness.
Ease of use: Easy.
Weight: Light to medium.

LOOSE-WEAVE SILK

Durable, rough silk fabrics are available in a range of textured weaves. Despite their thickness, loose weaves can be sufficiently flexible to handle easily.
Ease of use: Use with caution. Some types will tend to fray.
Weight: Medium.

TUSSAH SILK

A durable, matt, slubbed silk with a natural colour variation. Frays easily.
Ease of use: Easy.
Weight: Light to medium.
Avoid: Heavyweight types.

STRIPES, CHECKS AND SPOTS

Geometric patterns, such as stripes and checks, can be either woven into the fabric or printed on it, whereas dots are usually printed. With woven fabrics the colours appear equally bright on the reverse side, so either side may be used, but printed fabrics always have a paler, blurry, wrong side.

Small regular patterns, like those shown here, can provide a useful guide for stitching straight seams and/or spacing embroidery stitches. They combine well with plain fabrics and with more complicated prints.

WOVEN-STRIPE COTTON

Often sold for men's shirting, this woven cotton launders well.
Ease of use: Easy.
Weight: Light.

PRINTED-STRIPE COTTON

Striped fabrics are easy to combine with plain colours and other printed patterns. Launders well.
Ease of use: Easy.
Weight: Light.

COTTON GINGHAM

Different sizes of checks are available in several colours, always with white. Launders well.
Ease of use: Easy.
Weight: Light.

SEERSUCKER GINGHAM

The puckered texture of this fabric is permanent, and striped seersucker is also available. Launders well.
Ease of use: Easy.
Weight: Light.

SMALL POLKA-DOT COTTON PRINT

Tiny dot patterns are good for small patches.
Ease of use: Easy.
Weight: Light.

LARGE POLKA-DOT COTTON PRINT

Here the background is printed blue, with the dots left in white.

Ease of use: Easy.

Weight: Light.

MULTICOLOURED DOT COTTON/ POLYESTER PRINT

Large dot patterns may not suit very small patches.

Ease of use: Easy.

Weight: Light.

WOOLLEN TARTAN

Traditional tartan fabric is woven in wool or wool blends. Patterns may be small or large. Try choosing various areas of the woven pattern for different patches.

Ease of use: Use with caution. Large patterns can be dominant.

Weight: Light to medium.

Avoid: Heavyweight tartan.

COTTON CHECK

Often sold for casual shirts, small check patterns like this are easy to combine with other fabrics.

Ease of use: Easy.

Weight: Light to medium.

CHECK-AND-FLOWER WOVEN COTTON

Many patterns are available in woven cotton, such as this dress fabric, which would be suitable for a child's project.

Ease of use: Easy.

Weight: Light to medium.

PRINTED COTTONS

From floral designs and abstract patterns to children's prints, there are printed cotton fabrics to suit every taste and every project. As a rule, small all-over designs are easier to use than designs with large separate motifs. Combine complicated prints with plain fabrics, stripes or checks for a fresh, modern look.

TRADITIONAL BATIK COTTON

Traditional Indonesian batik designs feature flowers, leaves, butterflies and other subjects from the natural world.
Ease of use: Easy.
Weight: Light.

MODERN BATIK COTTON

Batik designs are formed by painting wax onto white fabric, then dying the fabric and removing the wax. The result is a loose hand-painted look.
Ease of use: Easy.
Weight: Light.

IKAT COTTON

The warp threads of ikat fabric are printed (or painted) before the weaving process begins, forming the characteristic blurry striped effect.
Ease of use: Easy.
Weight: Light.

ALL-OVER PRINTS

Medium-scale brightly coloured prints are available in a huge range of patterns and colourways. Choose two or three to set the theme for cotton patchwork and add complementary plain fabrics and stripes.
Ease of use: Easy.
Weight: Light.

INDIAN CHEESECLOTH BORDER PRINT

Sold for making skirts, this type of border print can be the source of several small patches, with varying patterns in coordinating colours.

Ease of use: Use with caution.
Weight: Very light.

SUBTLE, BLURRY PRINTS

Allover, small-scale prints like these will complement bolder patterns and plain fabrics. Also useful as a lining for quilted projects.

Ease of use: Easy.
Weight: Light.

TEDDY BEAR PRINT

A wide variety of motif prints are available, from carrots and tractors to teddy bears and dolls.

Ease of use: Use with caution. These prints should be used sparingly, perhaps as the centre patch in a crazy-log arrangement, and combined with blending plain fabrics and simple patterns.
Weight: Light.

BLUE DOGS PRINT

The random arrangement of these little dogs and flowers makes this fabric easy to combine with other prints and plain fabrics.

Ease of use: Easy.
Weight: Light.

SIMPLE FLORAL

Simple medium-sized floral prints are easy to combine with plain fabrics, stripes, checks and dots.

Ease of use: Easy.
Weight: Light.

LARGE FLORAL

Splashy, all-over prints are easier to combine than formal designs.

Ease of use: Don't allow the pattern to dominate; use with caution.
Weight: Light.

SMALL FLORAL

Tiny Victorian floral patterns are a traditional component of many types of patchwork.

Ease of use: Easy.
Weight: Light.

SPECIAL EFFECTS

Luxury fabrics, such as silks, satins and brocades, bring a touch of the exotic to crazy patchwork. Combine smooth, glowing silks with contrasting textures, such as velvet or lace, or use metallic fabrics to add glamour to your projects.

SILK DUPION

A softly shining silk with a thick, uneven texture.

Ease of use: Easy but tends to fray.

Weight: Light to medium.

SHOT SILK

This silk is woven with one colour for the warp and another for the weft.

Ease of use: Easy but tends to fray.

Weight: Light.

HABUTAI SILK

Habutai silk is one of the lightest weights of silk. When it is hand painted (as below), very delicate effects are obtained.

Ease of use: Use with caution due to delicate nature of fabric.

Weight: Very light.

DUCHESS SATIN

This smooth, lustrous satin is widely available, usually sold for evening and bridalwear.

Ease of use: Easy.

Weight: Medium.

SYNTHETIC SATIN

All types of silk and satin have synthetic/ man-made equivalents.

Ease of use: Use with caution as it can be slippery to handle and may tend to fray.

Weight: Light to medium.

SATIN BROCADE

Brocade is woven with jacquard designs, like these flowers and leaves.

Ease of use: Use with caution as it can be slippery to handle and may tend to fray.

Weight: Medium.

SARI SILK

Traditional Indian silks are often woven with a border pattern in metallic thread.

Ease of use: Easy.

Weight: Light to medium.

SILK VELVET

Hand-painted silk velvet is a beautiful fabric but is difficult to stitch.

Ease of use: Use with caution. Tack carefully and use a ballpoint machine needle, or stitch by hand.

Weight: Medium.

LACE FABRIC

Lace fabric will reveal the seam allowances through the pattern.

Ease of use: Use with caution; to avoid visible seam allowances, tack it flat onto plain fabric and treat the two layers as one.

Weight: Light.

METALLIC MESH

Use this fabric as you would lace fabric. **Ease of use:** Use with caution; back patches with plain fabric to hide the seam allowances.

Weight: Light.

FLORAL LAMÉ WEAVE

Metallic and plain fibres woven in a jacquard design are not hard-wearing.

Ease of use: Use with caution; frays easily.

Weight: Light.

DEVORÉ VELVET

The pattern is formed by etching away parts of the velvet pile, leaving visible the translucent areas of the woven backing.

Ease of use: Use with caution. Stitch as silk velvet (see opposite).

Weight: Light to medium.

METALLIC PRINTED COTTON

The wide range of metallic printed cottons available provides an easy way to add sparkle to your work because these fabrics handle just like cotton prints.

Ease of use: Easy.

Weight: Light.

GEOMETRIC LAMÉ WEAVE

This tiny woven pattern would combine easily with plain silks and satins.

Ease of use: Use with caution; frays easily.

Weight: Light.

PLAIN LAMÉ WEAVE

This plain lamé fabric is woven with metallic and cotton threads, making it quite easy to handle.

Ease of use: Easy.

Weight: Light.

LACE, RIBBONS, BRAIDS AND CORDS

Lace may range from simple broderie anglaise to luxurious handmade designs. Ribbons are made from many different fibres, from synthetic satin to velvet and silk. Braids are sewn flat to the fabric surface and may be woven, braided or prestitched into scroll patterns. Finally, cords are rounded and very strong, and used for ties and handles, or couched in place for decorative effect.

PREGATHERED LACE

Pregathered lace is ready for insertion into a patchwork seam.

Ease of use: Easy.

BRODERIE ANGLAISE

This lace is machine embroidered onto lightweight cotton fabric, with cutout holes.

Ease of use: Easy.

NET LACE (ALENÇON LACE)

This type of lace is embroidered onto a net background.

Ease of use: Easy.

COTTON LACE (TORCHON LACE)

This simple openwork lace may be made from cotton or linen.

Ease of use: Easy.

HANDMADE LACE

Handmade lace is expensive – unless you learn to make your own – but just a small scrap can add a beautiful finishing touch.

Ease of use: Easy.

GUIPURE LACE COLLAR

Ready-made lace collars and cuffs may still be found in fine department stores.

Ease of use: Easy.

SATIN RIBBON

Satin ribbon is usually shiny on one side and matt on the other. It can be slippery, so tack it firmly before stitching.

Ease of use: Easy.

GROSGRAIN RIBBON

The ribbed texture of this reversible durable ribbon makes it strong and very easy to apply. It is also ideal for tie fastenings.

Ease of use: Easy.

VELVET RIBBON

The reverse side of velvet ribbon is plain fabric.

Ease of use: Easy.

JACQUARD RIBBON

This satin ribbon is reversible, with the woven jacquard pattern appearing on both sides.

Ease of use: Easy.

CHECKED RIBBON

Ribbons may be woven in patterns of stripes and checks, usually reversible.

Ease of use: Easy.

FLOWER-PRINT RIBBON

Satin ribbons may also be printed, and a wide variety of patterns is available. These are not reversible.

Ease of use: Easy.

PICTURE RIBBON

Many different designs are available in the form of durable woven ribbons.

Ease of use: Easy.

RIC-RAC BRAID

This durable ric-rac braid may be made from cotton or synthetic fibres. Machine-stitch it in place along its centre.

Ease of use: Easy.

METALLIC SCROLL BRAID

Many types of delicate scroll braid are available. Narrow cords are prestitched into curved designs.

Ease of use: Use with caution; decorative rather than hard-wearing.

PLAITED BRAID

A flexible braid is suitable for sewing in curved lines.

Ease of use: Easy.

NARROW RAYON CORD

Firm, durable, rounded cords like these may be couched to fabric or used for tie fastenings.

Ease of use: Easy.

VINTAGE AND HEIRLOOM FABRICS

By shopping in bargain fabric stores and charity shops it is possible to build a stash of useful fabrics for a small outlay. Cotton shirts and tablecloths, quirky ties and printed handkerchiefs, or a store of vintage embroideries can all be utilized. You can also reuse fabrics from your own garments, whether they are outgrown or simply out of style, and acquire remnants from friends.

COTTON SHIRT

Garments such as men's shirts will yield a surprising amount of fabric. Simply cut them apart at the seams and discard any worn parts and doubled parts, such as collars and cuffs, but keep the buttons.

Ease of use: Easy.
Weight: Light.

NECKTIE

Men's neckties come in a wide range of patterns and fabrics, including fine silks. Unpick the long centre back seam and remove any lining and/or interlining.

Ease of use: Use with caution as the fabric can be slippery to handle.
Weight: Light.

COTTON JACQUARD TABLECLOTH

The pattern on this tablecloth is a complex jacquard weave, so the wrong side shows the colours reversed. Use both sides to cut coordinating patches.

Ease of use: Easy.
Weight: Medium.

STRIPED COTTON NAPKIN

This 1950s table napkin is woven in multicoloured stripes. The fabric is as good as new.

Ease of use: Easy.
Weight: Medium.

ANTIMACASSAR WITH TATTED BORDER

The homemade, tatted border on this chair back (antimacassar) is frayed at both ends, but the centre part could be used as a trim.

Ease of use: Easy.
Weight: Medium.

FLOWER EMBROIDERY

A small dressing-table mat, hand embroidered with simple flowers.

Ease of use: Easy.
Weight: Medium.

PRINTED SATIN REMNANT

A remnant from a bridesmaid's dress from the 1950s, this unusual printed satin fabric was stashed away for fifty years but is still as good as new.

Ease of use: Easy.
Weight: Light.

TIPS

- Preworn clothing should be washed and dried before being cut apart.
- Leave hems and borders attached if you are storing the fabric, since this helps to prevent fraying.
- When cutting patches from garments and household linens, discard any parts that are stained or worn, and any doubled parts, such as hems.
- Keep the buttons!

PARIS SCARF

This souvenir scarf would provide several themed patches. The buildings and the spotted background could be used together with other coordinating fabrics.

Ease of use: Easy.
Weight: Lightweight.

CREAM LACE REMNANT

This remnant is from a recent wedding dress. Such pieces will not be wasted if incorporated in your crazy patchwork, perhaps in a project to commemorate the wedding itself.

Ease of use: Use with caution (see Lace Fabric, page 147).
Weight: Light.

DONKEY EMBROIDERY

This linen dressing-table mat is perhaps forty years old. Such remnants of embroidery are often found in charity shops.

Ease of use: Easy.
Weight: Medium.

INITIALLED HANDKERCHIEF

This fragile silk handkerchief is worn at the edges, but the beautiful embroidered initial could be preserved and used as a patch in a decorative project.

Ease of use: Use with caution, decorative rather than hard-wearing.
Weight: Very light.

CROCHET DOILY

Hand crocheted in cotton yarn, sections of this circular doily could be used as trims in the same way as lace.

Ease of use: Use with caution. Paint cut edges with fabric glue to prevent unravelling.
Weight: Medium.

JAPANESE SCARVES

When travelling, look out for unusual fabrics, scarves, handkerchiefs, etc. These modern scarves were purchased in Tokyo.

Ease of use: Easy.
Weight: Medium.

TEMPLATES

Some of these project templates are shown full size while others require enlarging by the percentage given. Photocopy the templates onto thin card and cut them out with paper-cutting scissors.

POTHOLDER Back pocket

enlarge by photocopying at 200%

20cm (8 in.)

Potholder (page 38)

DRAWSTRING BAG BASE

enlarge by photocopying at 200%

radius 10.15 cm (4 in.)

*Drawstring bag
(page 44)*

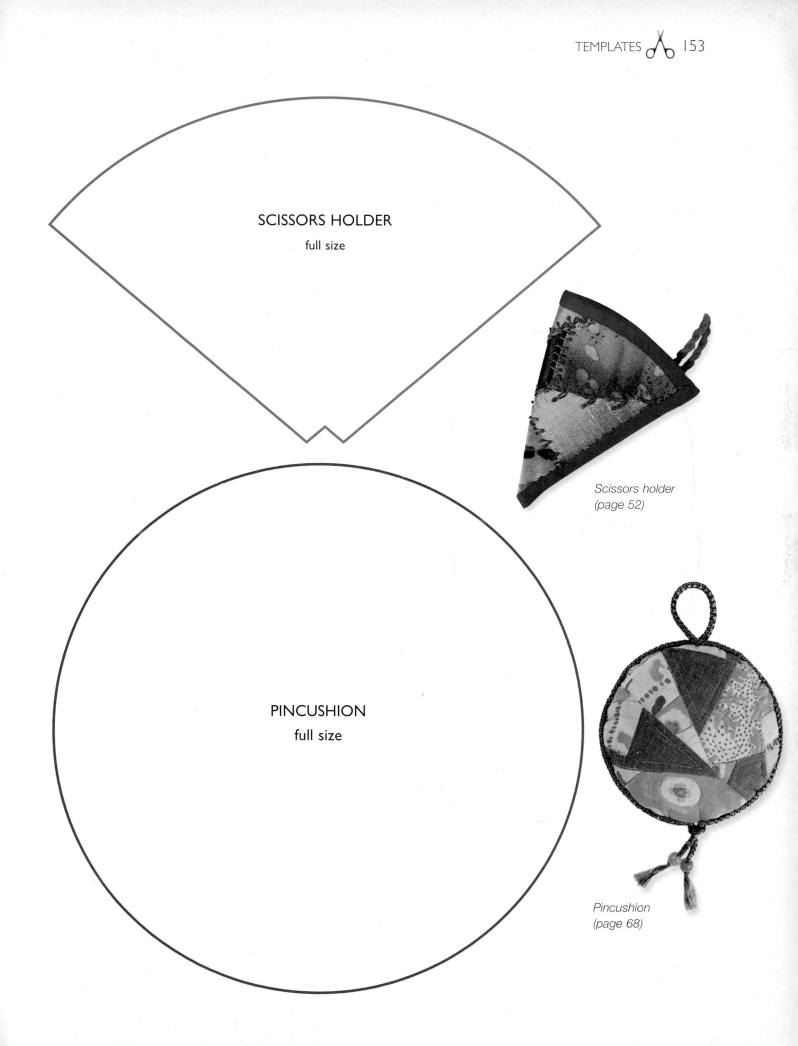

SCISSORS HOLDER

full size

*Scissors holder
(page 52)*

PINCUSHION

full size

*Pincushion
(page 68)*

Enlarge these pattern pieces by 150% on a photocopier.

Each small square is equal to 1 cm ($\frac{3}{8}$ in.).

If you don't have access to a photocopier you can copy the outlines by hand onto suitable graph paper.

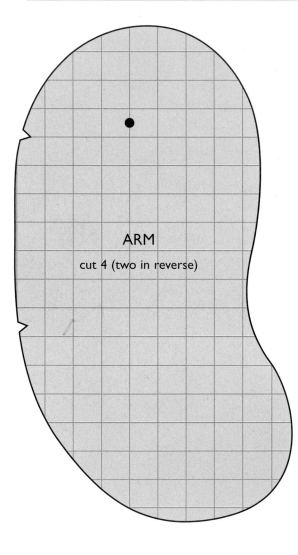

ARM

cut 4 (two in reverse)

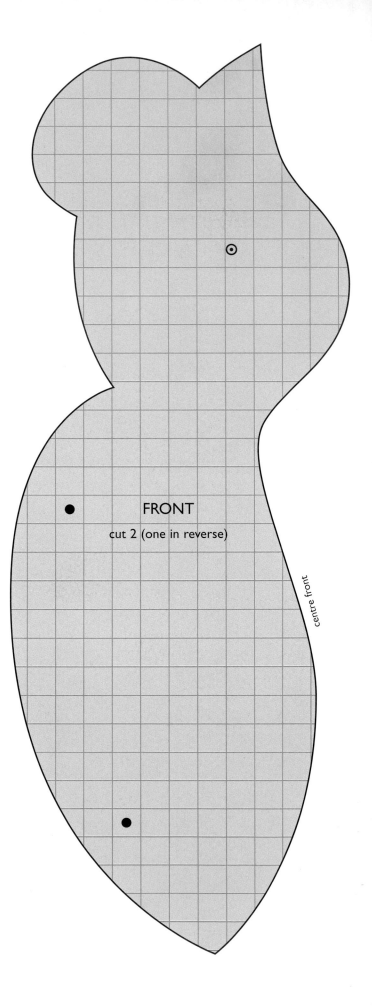

FRONT

cut 2 (one in reverse)

centre front

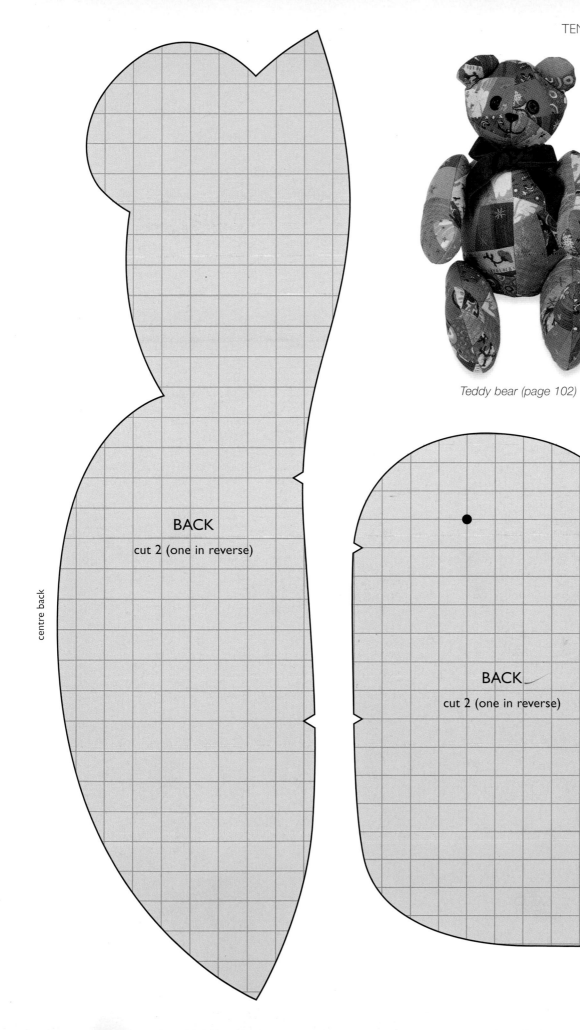

BACK

cut 2 (one in reverse)

centre back

Teddy bear (page 102)

BACK

cut 2 (one in reverse)

RESOURCES

Some websites listed below provide a mail-order service while others supply stockist information.

Barnyarns
Canal Wharf
Bondgate Green
Ripon
North Yorkshire
HG4 1AQ
+44 (0)1765 690 069
www.barnyarns.com
Sewing and embroidery threads and other sewing accessories

Coats Crafts UK
PO Box 22
Lingfield House
McMullen Road
Darlington
CO Durham
KL1 1YQ
+44 (0)1325 394 237
www.coatscrafts.co.uk
Fabrics, threads and accessories

Creative Grids Ltd
Unit 4
Swannington Road
Broughton Astley
Leicester
LE9 6TU
+44 (0)845 450 7722
www.creativegrids.com
Fusible-web and foundation papers

DMC Creative World
www.dmc.com
Embroidery threads

Dylon International Ltd
Worsley Bridge Road
Lower Sydenham
London
SE26 5HD
+44 (0)208 663 4801
www.dylon.co.uk
Photo-transfer paste and paper

Fabric Heaven
1B Ferozeshah Road
Devizes
Wiltshire
SN10 2JQ
+44 (0)1380 722 597
www.fabricheaven.net
Man-made dupions, satins and bridal fabrics

Gutermann
www.guetermann.com
Machine-embroidery threads

Kate's Kloths
58 Regent Street
Blyth
Northumberland
NE24 1LT
+44 (0)1670 354 342
www.kateskloths.co.uk
Hand-dyed threads, ribbons, silk and velvet fabrics

Lazertran
+44 (0)1545 571 149
www.lazertran.com
Photo-transfer papers

Makower UK

118 Greys Road

Henley-on-Thames

Oxfordshire

RG9 1QW

+44 (0)1491 413 401

www.makoweruk.com

Cotton print fabrics

Rowan

Green Lane Mill

Holmfirth

HD9 2DX

+44 (0)1484 681 881

www.knitrowan.com

Plain and printed cotton fabrics

Nevtex On-line Shop

+44 (0)115 959 8781

www.nevtex.co.uk

Beads, sequins, lace and

party fabrics

Patchwork Corner

51 Belswains Lane

Hemel Hempstead

Herts

HP3 9PW

+44 (0)1442 259 000

www.patchworkcorner.co.uk

Fabrics and notions for quilting

Pearsall's

Tancred Street

Taunton

Somerset

TA1 1RY

+44 (0)1823 274 700

www.pearsallsembroidery.co.uk

Silk embroidery threads

Quilt Direct

Peter Tavy

Tavistock

Devon

PL19 9NA

+44 (0)1822 810 877

www.quiltdirect.co.uk

Batting, threads and stabilizers

The Cotton Patch

1285 Stratford Road

Hall Green

Birmingham

B28 9AJ

+44 (0)121 7022 840

www.cottonpatch.net

Patchwork and quilting fabrics

The Quilt Room

20 West Street

Dorking

Surrey

RH4 1BL

+44 (0)1306 740 739

www.quiltroom.co.uk

Patchwork and quilting supplies

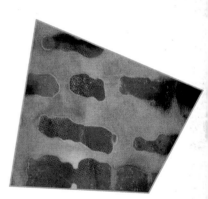

The Silk Route

Cross Cottage

Cross Lane

Frimley Green

Surrey

GU16 6LN

+44 (0)1252 835 781

www.thesilkroute.co.uk

Silk fabrics

Whaleys (Bradford) Ltd

Harris Court

Great Horton

Bradford

West Yorkshire

BD7 4EQ

+44 (0)1274 576 718

Cotton, linen and silk fabrics

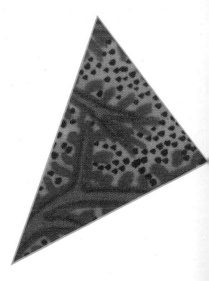

Vilene

www.vilene.com

Stabilizers and batting

INDEX

CREDITS

Author Acknowledgements

The author would like to thank Claire Rowan for making the chair pillow and baby quilt projects on pages 76 and 96. Thanks also to the Rowan Fabric Collection for supplying many of the plain and printed cotton fabrics used throughout the book.

Picture Credits